Transgender Rights
Identity and Mobility

Transgender Rights Identity and Mobility

Edited by

Dr. Madhusudhan B

KALPAZ

First Published, 2021

Published by

Kalpaz Publications
C-30, Satyawati Nagar,
Delhi – 110052
Ph.: 011-47034999, 9811692060
www.kalpazpublications.com
E-mail: kalpaz@hotmail.com

Printed at: Gyan Press, Delhi.

Cataloging in Publication Data—DK
Courtesy: D.K. Agencies (P) Ltd. <docinfo@dkagencies.com>

Transgender rights identity and mobility / [editor], Dr. Madhusudhan B.
pages cm
Contributed articles.
Includes bibliographical references and index.
ISBN 9789353246129

1. Transgender people—Legal status, laws, etc.—India. 2. Transgender people—Legal status, laws, etc.—India—Kerala. 3. Transgender people—India—Identity. 4. Transgender people—India—Kerala—Identity. I. Madhusudhan, B., 1967- editor.

LCC KNS2107.G38T73 2021 | DDC 342.54087 23

Contents

List of Contributors

Karthika, K: *Assistant Professor, PG Department of Commerce, NSS Hindu College, Changanacherry, Kottayam, Kerala*

Nikhil, S.: *M Com Student, NSS Hindu College, Changanacherry, Kottayam, Kerala*

Dr. Jayasankar, K.I: Assistant Professor, Department of Law, Central University of Kerala

Anagh: Research Scholar, Mahatma Gandhi University, Kottayam

Dr. Mohan Varughese: Associate Professor and Head Department of Political Science, Mar Thoma College, Thiruvalla, Kerala, India

Krupa Susan Varghese: Post – Graduate Scholar, Department of Geopolitics and International Relations, Manipal Academy of Higher Education (MAHE), Manipal, Karnataka, India

Sunil Mohan: Assistant Professor, Department of History, NSS Hindu College, Changanacherry

Nayana, BS: Assistant Professor, NSS Hindu College, Changanacherry

Lijitha: Research Scholar, School of International Relations, Central University of Kerala, Kasagode

Dr. R.S. Vineeth: Assistant Professor, Dept. of History, NSS Hindu College, Changanacherry

Dr. Nisha Jolly Nelson: Asst. Professor & Head, Department of Sociology, Loyola College of Social Sciences, Sreekariyam, Thiruvananthapuram, Email: nishanelson@gmail.com

Athira, G.J.: Assistant Professor, Dept. of Commerce, NSS Hindu College, Changancherry

Anu Kuriakose: Research Scholar, Dept. of Humanities, IIST, Thiruvananathapuram

Vinshi, P.K.: Research Scholar, Dept. of Political Science, University of Kerala, Karyavattom

Dr. Thomas Joseph: Vice Principal Assumption College, Changanacherry

Soumya, S: Assistant Professor, Department of Political Science, NSS Hindu College, Changanacherry

Parvathy, N.S.: Assistant Professor, Department of Political Science, NSS Hindu College, Changanacherry

Rajagopal, P.K.: Assistant Professor, Post Graduate Department of Political Science, NSS Hindu College, Changanacherry, Kerala.

Karthika, K.: Assistant Professor, PG Department of Commerce, NSS Hindu College, Changanacherry, Kottayam, Kerala

Nikhil, S.: M Com Student, NSS Hindu College, Changanacherry, Kottayam, Kerala

1

Transgenders in India-Legally Recognised and Socially Reprobated

— Dr. Jayasankar, K.I

Introduction

There are persons in our society whose gender identity, gender expression or behaviour does not conform to the sex to which they were assigned at birth. These persons are brought under an umbrella term 'Transgender'. Transgender is an individual who presents themself and lives as a gender that does not corresponds with the sex they were assigned at birth.[1] When gender identity relates to a person's internal sense of being male, female or something else, gender expression refers to the way a person communicates gender identity to others through behaviour, clothing, hairstyles, voice or body characteristics.

The ways that transgender people are talked about in popular culture, academia and science are constantly changing, particularly as individuals' awareness, knowledge and openness about transgender people and their experiences grow.[2] Transgender people have existed in every culture, race, and class since the story of human life has been recorded. That includes people who do not self-identify as transgender, but who are seems as such by others and thus are subject to the same social oppressions and physical violence. Though the transgender, in our society, encompass all races, ethnicity, religious and social classes, they've never enjoyed a respectable life, because of "what they are" and "how they are".[3]

Transgenders in India: Legally recognised under constitutional safeguards

A transgender in India is included within the words "any person" and is given equal status to that of every cis-gender in India.Transgender community includes Hijras, Eunuchs, Kothis, Aravanis, Jogappas, Shiv Shakthis etc., who have been a part of Indian society for centuries. The Vedic and Puranic literatures mention "tritiya prakriti" meaning the third gender and "napunsaka" meaning someone with the loss of procreative ability. The word hijra used in the Indian language appears to be derived from the Persian word hiz, i.e., someone who is effeminate and/or ineffective or incompetent. Another commonly used word is kinnar, whereas chhakka is used in a derogatory context.[4]

Preamble to the Constitution secures to all citizens equality of status and opportunity. It mandates Justice- social, economic and political. Accordingly the first and foremost right that they are deserving is the right to equality.[5] Article 15 speaks about the prohibition of discrimination on the ground of religion, race, caste, sex or place of birth.Under Article 19(1)(a) certain basic freedoms, which constitute as human rights, are granted as natural rights to all the citizens of India including, right to freedom of speech and expression of his self-identified gender and the right to choose one's personal appearance. Though the values of privacy, self-identity, autonomy and personal integrity are guaranteed to the members of the transgender community under it and the state is bound to protect and recognise these rights, but in many cases, there exists a disassociation between their gender, their social name and their identification documents which dehumanises them and also denies them their civil and legal status.[6] The greatest and most inclusive constitutional provision is Article 21 which states that no person shall be deprived of life or personal liberty except according to procedure established by law commonly understood as "Right to life", which includes within it self-determination of gender which is an integral part of personal autonomy. However, somehow we have failed in letting the people with alternate sexualities live a life with respect and dignity. Article 21 ensures right to privacy and personal dignity to all the citizens. Article 23 prohibits trafficking in human beings as beggars and other similar forms of forced labour and any contravention of these provisions shall be an offence punishable in accordance with law.

Judiciary on Transgenders Right

Transgenders have been demanding for a life of decency, certainty and respect in independent India for over seven decades now. A turning point happened in the history of transgender rights in India was in July 2009. The Delhi High Court in *Naz Foundation vs Government of Delhi*[7] on 2nd July 2009, ended over a century of discriminatory treatment against people because of their sexual orientation by declaring the application of significant elements of Section 377 of the Indian Penal Code (IPC) unconstitutional decriminalised homosexuality allowing consensual sex between two homosexuals as long as they are above the legal age of 18 years.The decision brought Indian jurisprudence into conformity with international law by decriminalising all consensual same sex activity between adults.

As the Court noted:

> "In our view, Indian Constitutional law does not permit the statutory criminal law to be held captive by the popular misconceptions of who the LGBTs are. It cannot be forgotten that discrimination is antithesis of equality and that it is the recognition of equality which will foster the dignity of every individual."

"The Court stated that Section 377 of the Indian Penal Code was violative of Article 14 (Right to Equality), Article 15 (Prohibition of discrimination) and Article 21 (Protection of life and personal liberty). The judges in the right constitutional spirit stated that 'the criminal law cannot be held captive by the popular misconceptions of who the lesbian, gay, bi-sexual, transgenders (LGBTs) are'. In 2013, in the *Suresh Koushal vs. Naz Foundation* case Mr. Suresh Kaushal, an astrologer argued that homosexuality could even pose danger to national security as the soldiers fighting at the borders could be tempted to take male lovers and India might lose a battle because of that.[8] In a regressive order, the Supreme Court set aside the 2009 order asserted that Section 377 affects only a 'miniscule' population in India and does not suffer from the constitutional infirmity and the Delhi High Court judgment is legally unsustainable. This was a huge blow for the transgenders who felt confidence to assert their identities after the 2009 judgment.

In 2014, the Supreme Court ruled that transgender people be recognised as a third gender and enjoy all fundamental rights.[9] In *NALSA* a bench of Justice K.S. Radhakrishnan and Justice A.K. Sikri passed a judgement holding that transgender persons have the fundamental right to self-identify their gender as male, female or transgender even without medical reassessment. The Court noted that the transgender community (broadly defined by the Court to include Hijras, eunuchs, Kothis, Aravanis and numerous others) has faced prejudice and disadvantage since the eighteenth century in India. It acknowledged the discrimination that transgender people face in areas of life including healthcare, employment and education, which often leads to social exclusion. The Court declared that numerous steps were necessary in order for centre and state governments to comply with the constitutional rights to life, equality before the law, non-discrimination and freedom of expression.The governments were asked to take steps for the welfare of transgender persons and to treat them as a third gender for the purpose of safeguarding their fundamental rights. The Court held that the right to express one's identity in a non-binary gender was an essential part of freedom of expression. The judgment gave directives that all kinds of reservation should be extended to transgenders in educational institutions and for public appointments. Pursuant to the judgment, the third gender category on identity documents such as passport and voter's card has begun to make an appearance.

In the year 2017 another judgement was pronounced by the Supreme Court in *Puttaswamy vs. Union of India*[10] in which the Court held that there is a constitutional right to privacy inherent in the right to life, equality and fundamental freedoms.The court has rightly pointed out that the right to privacy specifically includes the right to have intimate relations of one's choice and the right to sexual orientation and gender identity.

While recognising the right of transgenders of self-determination of their sex, the Court explained the contours of human dignity in the following words:

> "The basic principle of the dignity and freedom of the individual is common to all nations, particularly those having democratic set up. Democracy requires us to respect and develop the free spirit of human being which is responsible for all progress in human history. Democracy is also a method by which we attempt to raise the living standard of the people and to give opportunities to every person to develop his/her personality. It is founded on peaceful co-existence and cooperative living. If democracy is based on the recognition of the individuality and dignity of man, as a fortiori we have to recognise the right of a human being to choose his sex/gender identity which is integral to his/her personality and is one of the most basic aspect of self-determination, dignity and freedom. In fact, there is a growing recognition that the true measure of development of a nation is not economic growth; it is human dignity.

Subsequently in *Navtej Johar*[11], the court has found special relevance for transgender Rights. In this case the court has gone far beyond the anti-sodomy judgements from around the world that were refered to it. The court has recognised the aspects of gender identity and sexual orientation and acknowledged the voices of the most vulnerable sexual minorities within the LGBTQ community and took the stand that the constitution protects the rights of all.

Legislative attempt to protect Transgender's Rights

There are different laws enacted by legislature as the outcome of constitutional provisions to establish the right in favour of transgender community. In August 2016 the Transgender Persons (Protection of Rights) Bill, 2016 was introduced in the parliament seeking to define transgenders and prohibit discrimination against them.[12] This Bill came two years after the landmark *NALSA* judgment of 2014 which recognised the fundamental rights of transgender persons and gave broad directives to the government to facilitate the realisation of these rights.

But this legislation is also not free from the criticisms. It is argued that this bill does not define the term discrimination as was given in 2014 Bill.[13] It laid down discrimination as distinction, exclusion, or restriction on the basis of gender identity. The 2016 Bill completely eliminates the option of identification as either male or female. On top of it, the Bill reinforces injurious stereotypes about transgender persons as being part male and part female.[14] After two years the Bill was passed by the Lok Sabha (Lower House of Indian Parliament) on 17 December, 2018. The 2018 Bill, if adopted, would effectively deny to most transgender people their right to self-identification, by providing an overly complex bureaucratic procedure requiring an individual's application for a transgender certificate to be approved by two different sets of authorities, despite earlier widespread condemnation of this process by the transgender community.[15]

Transgender in India: socially reprobated

But the transgender community continues to be ostracised. They are marginalised, abused, scorned and callously neglected community in India.[16] The Constitution affirms equality in all spheres but the moot question is whether it is being applied. Identification on the basis of sex within male and female is a crucial component of civil identity as required by the Indian state. The Indian state's policy of recognising only two sexes and refusing to recognise hijras as women, or as a third sex (if a hijra wants it), has deprived them at a stroke of several rights that Indian citizens take for granted. These rights include the right to vote, the right to own property, the right to marry, the right to claim a formal identity through a passport and a ration card, a driver's licence, the right to education, employment, health and so on. Such deprivation secludes hijras from the very fabric of Indian civil society.

Conclusion

Inspite of Indian society's spirit of tolerance and acceptance, there appears to be limited public knowledge and understanding of same sex, sexual orientation and people whose gender identity and expression are incongruent with their biological sex. Attrocities and human rights violations against the transgender communities in India have been widely documented.Over 40 percent of Indian women according to the Human Development Report's Gender Inequality Index[17] suffers abuse, neglect or violence at the hands of their husbands or family members. Girl child rape is at an all-time high. Even now it appears very difficult for the families to accept if their male child starts behaving in ways that are considered feminine or inappropriate to the expected gender role. More over these family members may threaten, scold or even abuse their male children from behaving or dressing-up like a girl or woman. In a nutshell, to protect sexual minorities including transgenders from crimes and abuse against them we required to strengthen their voices, frame policies that push for intervention and systematise our social justice mechanisms.

References

1. *See* "LGBT Terms and Definitions." *Spectrum Center University of Michigan*, 12 Nov. 2016.
2. https://www.apa.org/topics/lgbt/transgender.aspx
3. Madhana, B, 'Third Gender Rights: Emerging Trends & Issues', The World Journal on Juristic Polity, March, 2017. ISSN: 2394-5044.
4. Michelraj, M. 'Historical evolution of transgender community in India', Asian Rev Soc. Sci 2015; 4:17-9.
5. Article-14 of Constitution of India. The state shall not deny to any person equality before the law or the equal protection of the laws within the territory of India.
6. Prof. Shilpa Khatri Babbar,'The Socio-Legal Exploitation of the Third Gender in India', IOSR Journal of Humanities and Social Science (IOSR-JHSS) Volume 21, Issue 5, Ver. 4 (May. 2016) pp. 12-18 e-ISSN: 2279-0837, p-ISSN: 2279-0845.
7. 160 Delhi Law Times 277.
8. 'It is like reversing the motion of the earth'; The Hindu; December 20, 2013 http://www.thehindu.com/features/metroplus/society/it-is-like-reversing-the-motion-of-theearth/article5483306.ece
9. *National Legal Service Authority v. Union of India,* AIR 2014 SC 1863, (2014) 5 SCC 438.
10. https://indiankanoon.org/doc/127517806/
11. *Navtej Singh Johar & Ors. v. Union of India thr. Secretary Ministry of Law and Justice*, W. P. (Crl.) No. 76 of 2016 (Supreme Court of India).
12. https://www.indiatoday.in/india/story/lok-sabha-passes-transgender-rights-bill-1411420-2018-12-17.

13. The right of Trangender Persons Bill 2014.
14. *The New Transgender Bill Fails the Community*, https://thewire.in/gender/failures-of-the-newtransgender- bill two different sets of authorities, despite earlier widespread condemnation of this process by the transgender community15.
15. https://www.icj.org/india-parliament-must-revise-problematic-transgender-persons-protection-of-rights-bill-2018/
16. Sibsankar Mal, 'Let Us to Live: Social Exclusion of Hijra Community', Asian Journal of Research in Social Sciences and Humanities, Vol. 5, No. 4, April 2015, pp. 108-117.
17. The Gender Inequality Index (GII) is an index for measurement of gender disparity that was introduced in the 2010 Human Development Report 20th anniversary edition by the United Nations Development Programme (UNDP).

2

State Policy for Transgenders in Kerala 2015 as a Kerala Model of Development

—*Anagh*

Transgender community is one of the major marginalised groups, recorded with discrimination living in the outskirts of the mainstream society in the different corners of the world. Nations like Australia, Finland, New Zealand, Sweden, Mexico, Austria, South Africa, etc. have taken various steps and policies which ensure equality and justice or the inclusion of gender and sexuality minorities in the mainstream society. Movements like Gay Liberation Front and Gay Activists' Alliance in the mid-1950s, National Bisexual Liberation Group in the early 1980s from the different parts of the world paved the way for their recognition nationally as well as internationally. Those demands prompted United Nations, Amnesty International, etc. to take up necessary steps and constitute certain policies which protect the rights of the sexuality minority globally. Along with that there are quite a lot of movements in various parts demanded for their rights and dignities, brought new policies and laws in different nations which ensure betterment in their social life. But their condition and the mainstream community's perceptions on them still remain unchanged. They are still living in the peripheries of the mainstream society, other admidst taboos.

Revolutionary judgement of Delhi High Court in 2009 decriminalised homosexuality and forwarded to the Indian Parliament to amend IPC 377. The verdict from the Delhi High Court recognised the right of all the sexuality minorities to live peacefully by disclosing their sexuality. But, in 2013, Supreme Court came up with another judgement which recriminalised homosexuality and the life of the homosexuals in India was under question again until the decriminalisation of IPC 377 came out in September 6, 2018. The NALSA judgement of 2014 April was the first verdict well defined that elevated the status of gender and sexuality minorities. As per the recommendations of the *Union v/s NALSA* judgement of 2014, all the state governments where supposed to take actions and formulate policies and laws to ensure the betterment of conditions of Transgender people in socio-economic and cultural realms.[1]

The Union v/s National Legal Services Authority (NALSA) verdict of 15th April 2014 gave citizenship to the Transgender community. The above mentioned verdict was influenced by a written petition filed by National Legal Services Authority on 15 April, 2014. After it was filed, a Member of Parliament from Tamil Nadu, Tiruchi Shiva, introduced a private bill in the Parliament in 2014 which in fact passed unanimously by all members in the Indian Parliament. This bill aimed to deceive all the inequalities faced by the Transgender community. The Supreme Court and the Private Bill proposed to establish commissions and policy framing mechanisms when it comes to the issues that are related to Transgenders. The Central Social Welfare Department had a plan to make some corrections in the bill that was already introduced in Rajya Sabha and re-introduced it in Parliament. The states are also framing policies in the trajectory.[2]

The policy of the Kerala Social Justice Department has already included this matter through deliberations and debates with and between intellectuals whose thoughts are scattered towards this issue. In this light, social justice department of Kerala government formulated State Policy for Transgenders in Kerala, 2015. The definition given to the transgender is the gender which has been opted by the person against their sex. This can be male to female or female to male.

In Kerala, as per the survey conducted by the Social Justice Department, there are 25,000 Transgender people. But as the society is still transphobic, and faces discrimination in all walks of their life, most of them do not declare their identity. The present transgender policy of 2015 ensures and guarantees rights of transgender community. Fundamental rights guaranteed by constitution i.e., equality and equity irrespective of gender, freedom of expression, and right to dignified life are the backbone of the State Policy for Transgenders in Kerala, 2015. As per the recommendation of the Supreme Court, transgender community is to be considered for reservation in the field of education, employment and other necessary fields for the betterment and mainstreaming.

Definition of the problem

The situation in Kerala society or of the mind-set of the people leads to catastrophic but the sincerity behind the measures taken by the government is to appreciate. Activists says that many projects initiated by the government and its agencies were still remaining on paper. Taking the instance of this - World- wide publicity was given to the appointment of 23 transgender people gave Kochi Metro Rail Limited (KMRL). It was the first time a government run entity in India hired transgender people as employees. The publicity has ironically confounded the miseries of the sexual minority even as various international agencies and media hailed it as a path-breaking initiative. While some of the transgender people who were living in the state by hiding their real sexual identity, were forced to leave their homes, facing difficulty in finding alternate accommodation in the city. Many of them tried to stick on with the job but found it hard to continue the service, not because they were not satisfied with their job due to the social stigma that refused to go away, even in a progressive society like Kerala, as it became increasingly difficult for them to find accommodations.

The transgender community joy knew no bounds when they received the appointment from KMRL. But their joy short-lived after they could not find a place to sleep in the city. Faizal Faizu, who has been trying to stick on with the job, said he was staying in a lodge paying Rs 600 per day. The situation was more plight when many of them were forced to get into sex work on to their job.

At this point of time doubts the sincerity behind the measures taken by the government. He said many projects initiated by the government and its agencies were still remaining on paper. Though the Kerala was the first state in India to bring out a policy for transgender people, the approaches of the society as well as some government has brought, transgender policies, the current Left government has allocated Rs 20 crore in the three successive budgets to fund development initiatives for transgender community.

It is a classic case of everything looking bright on paper but less so on the ground, says J. Devika, a writer and associate professor on gender at the Thiruvananthapuram-based Center for Development Studies.

The problems faced by Transgender community do not limit back of accommodation alone. They are exploited and abused in public places like railway stations, bus stands, schools, workplaces, malls, theatres and hospitals. They face a huge amount of human rights violation. They are even side-lined and treated as untouchables. They are the ones who are always blamed when anything happens at the work place where the transgender people also work. The instance of the accusing a transgender employee when a cash storage was found at the ticket counter of KMRL at Edappally station, was infamous.

Hypothesis

The quality of Transgender people's life in Kerala is good and is becoming better after the Transgender policy of 2014.

The policies implement by the present LDF lead government bring in more policies that makes Kerala transgender friendly.

Methodology

The main aim of the study is to find out the quality of life of transgender in Kerala. The study used one on one interview with a schedule. The study was conducted in districts in Kerala. The KASACS projects reports 2016 show that there are about 25,000 transgender are in the state but the majority of them are more or less invisible in mainstream society. The respondents who have given their interpretation and shared their experiences are majorly prominent transgender activists, both transmen and transwomen. The researcher met with several transgender organisations that work for the uplift and rights of the transgender people. There wasn't any sample size, however the researcher had met and talked to 10 transgender people and some people who are gender non-confirming transgender community in the state.

Observation

In accordance with the estimates formulated in relation to demographic transition, the population classified under other or "Third gender" has been underestimated. "Third genders have mostly identified in the Indian census of 2011. Trans-men or binary transwomen have not been included in the census of 2011. Non-confirming population with respect to gender have not been identified and included there in.

As far as the transgender people based in the state of Kerala are concerned, financial independence, educational background as well as accomplishments or achievements have provided a boost to their socio-economic existence in general.

The first state to announce a transgender policy, Kerala, has taken another step to include transgender persons in the mainstream by announcing reservation for students pursuing degree in the Arts and Sciences.

The government has directed all state and affiliated universities to reserve two seats for transgender students in undergraduate and post graduate courses subject to fulfilment of qualification. It has also directed these institutions to ensure that transgender students are not discriminated against in any manner. An order issued by their department of higher education stated, “Due to social issues and pressure these students are often forced to discontinue their studies.”

Result

Social stigma and taboo still remains and the atrocities and discrimination lead to peaceless life of the community in the society.

When comes to health sector, there still remains a lot of discrimination. As noted above, the SRS Department is absent in Kerala. As elucidate above, there is no palliative care facility for the transgender.

Education sector is furthermore developed and friendly. The 2% reservation shows that the education is open to all, irrespective of gender.

Transgender ID card distribution has many flaws in the implementation.

Transgender boards in the district is not functioning, as it was supposed too.

Statistics shows that, when comes to visibility, after the policies implemented in 2016, the coming out with proper identity is more. This shows that Kerala is now more transgender friendly. Likewise, the transgender people, who went outside Kerala for better living, is coming back to Kerala.

Further policies, yet to implement, make Kerala more Transgender friendly, like monetary help for self-employment, etc.

The policies explained further before, show that community is getting more recognition and acceptance. This shows that transphobia in the government is getting reduced.

Suggestion

The transgender ID card takes a lot of time and it is the primary proof for the community people to get any service. Till the Transgender card gets delivered, the receipt of the card may be considered as a proof or identity.

The social stigma should be reduced and gradually removed. More gender sensitisation programmes are to be conducted.

As elucidated in the project, the inclusion of gender studies and the study on LGBTQIA+ is to be included in the education curriculum since 7th standard and even in B.Ed.

Gender awareness should be given to police officers and doctors.

Data Interpretation and Conclusion

Inclusion with respect to Healthcare the term implies the status of providing of amenities of healthcare inclusion of transgender/ intersex ensuring equal opportunities and support in this guard. The facilities/amenities of healthcare to be made readily available, in accordance with the policies or directives framed by the Government from time to time. Activities initiated in this direction, whatsoever, should be devoid of any kind of discrimination towards transgender/intersex, as has deliberated at length in the previous chapters. The policies and programmes /steps undertaken by the Govt. to ensure services to transgender free from any kind of discrimination should be viewed seriously in relation to the services/amenities being made available to them. In other words the services provided should be devoid of fear or favour, and must be at par with policies envisaged by the government in this regard. Medical practitioners, specialists, administrators and all others involved in the stream are to take due note of the above and eradicate all kinds of traditional beliefs/apprehensions in dealing with matters relating to transgender/intersex. After all, they form the biological group of 'homosapience'! They too owe a right to live!

Adequate care is to be taken in case of serious illness/conditions of health relating to old age/pecuniary conditions of being bedridden/first aid in case of cardio-vascular and other diseases etc. Timely check-up, medical follow-up, medical review, medication facilities under the advice of specialists is to be ensured along with life-saving methods is to be made available, if warranted. Palliative care is also to be ensured, in case of need the same needs to be assessed/reviewed from time to time, in the light of demands on the basis of health of the patient. At this juncture, it is important to note that transgender/intersex have been subjected to intense deprivation and it is important that their interests/ demands are being safeguarded. There have been cases of refusal of treatment to transgender people by doctors of reputed private hospitals in the recent past. In addition, charging of more amount as fees, in comparison to their male and female counter-parts, though sounds incredible, is a true incident which has been a recent occurrence. Furthermore, it is to mention that it is not the doctors alone who go in on unhealthy and unscientific apprehensions, but also the team of workers behind the whole frame work of action.

We, as citizens of this great country of ours, have committed ourselves to the march towards a better tomorrow. As I move towards the conclusion of my project, I cannot but present this question. Are such kinds of activities conducive towards a better outlook on human welfare?

Special consideration towards the interests of transgender/intersex in the light of the deprivation undergone by transgender or intersex over a long gestation period, there is no shadow of doubt that it's the dawn of a new era, of the eradication of traditional beliefs, thus, the birth of a new age, devoid of any kind of discrimination. In the decision to include our own fraternity into our own community. This effort of mine is but a beginning, with a little consideration so special, so valuable for them transgender our own brethren!

The onset of gender discrimination has been the resultant of the traditional beliefs, of the existence of only the male and female as two genders created since time immemorial by way of our own thought, and that of the society, as well. The passage of time, however, has shaped the roots of thought a day filled with hope of a better future. Efforts in this direction a kindled a ray of hope, a spark of satisfaction, of inclusion of transgender or intersex as a gender, in addition to their male and female counterparts. The state of Kerala has been accredited with appreciable efforts towards the providing of equal opportunities and recognition of transgender or intersex.

There have been instances in the previous years, when transgender or intersex were relegated to the background. They were denied opportunities of equal participation as a result of being the 'third gender' has, however, been eradicated and replaced by transgender people or intersex. Radha, a student, was a sportsperson and joined The Electricity Board in that category. Later, on being identified as a transgender, Radha, who, was changed to Radhakrishnan in the meantime, was denied the opportunity to continue in service. The same has been the case of MANU changed to Vijaya Raja Mallika, who has been out of employment, after being categorised as a transgender or transwoman in Kerala. It is a sad plight that Vijaya Raja Mallika has been a victim of such experiences, despite being a rank-holder in her collegiate education.

Traditional apprehensions as regards transgender people or intersex form the basis of the hazards or hindrances in social inclusion suffered by them. Barriers in social inclusion include barriers in education or employment or further prospects of freedom to lead a happy contended life. How to eke out a living? Despite policies and programmes framed thereunder, transgender people experience a sense of deprivation. The marginalisation of the marginalised is on the vogue. Participation in socio-economic and cultural issues, equal opportunities in respect of education, healthcare and employment is the need of the hour, in as far as transgender people are concerned. They are no longer dancers in family functions, as had been noticed in the outskirts of Kolkata, decades ago. This calls for a much broader outlook, a radiance of acceptance into the mainstream of social activities. Such acceptance would lend a helping hand towards their socio-cultural and economic upliftment. This would remove the stigma, hitherto embedded in the mindset of transgender people, proving to be hazardous towards their development. A new chapter in the lives of transgender people- a new shape to our own community, our own people. Several voluntary organisations have extended their valuable services in this direction, in the state of Kerala.

At this juncture, it is to be cited that the recognition sought for by transgender people is the result of strenuous efforts of transgender themselves. Who else, but themselves, can be a better identity to their sufferings? Sheethal Shyam, Vijaya Raj Mallika are some of the few transgender people who have been instrumental in this direction. After the appointment of 13 transgender people in Kochi Metro, they had to suffer, yet being devoid of rented houses, which, they were denied. As a consequence, they had to fall prey to sex rackets. They were considered as beggars by a large section of the population.

Bureaucrats declared their total ignorance of the existence of transgender people in Kerala. In such a condition, what steps can be initiated towards the welfare of transgender people by them?

It is a sad plight that transgender people had been subjected to stripping, as against constitutional norms. Today, stripping is taboo, instead, the declaration by the transgender, to the effect of being a transgender suffices. A survey conducted on transgender people revealed that most of them were drop-outs after ninth standard consequent of their non-inclusion either, along with male or the female. Being neither of the sexes, as defined vis-à-vis traditional sense, equality, fraternity etc as defined in the constitutional framework, had been taboo for transgender people as has been deliberated in this project, it goes without saying that transgender people or intersex have been subjected to untold suffering by their own families, and by the society as well. Untold misery and poverty, unemployment etc have compelled them to resort to begging and other unwarranted means of living. It is hoped that this humble effort of mine would be an eye-opener for the society, towards their upliftment and increased welfare. An emphatic action is warranted for better and improved results in this regard.

Notes

1. ihttps://www.thehindu.com/society/its-been-a-long-long-time-for-the-lgbtq-rights-movement-inindia/ article24408262.ece
2. https://www.thehindu.com/society/its-been-a-long-long-time-for-the-lgbtq-rights-movement-inindia/ article24408262.ece

References

1. Resmi, G. KS Anilkumar, "Transgender: charithramsamskaaramprathinidhanam." Chintha Publishers, Second Edition. 2016. Thiruvananthapuram
2. Judgement of NALSA v/s Union of India of the year 2014.
3. State Policy for Transgenders in Kerala, 2015.
4. Transgender survey Kerala 2014-2015 by the Social Justice Department of Kerala.
5. Centre for Development Studies, "Human Diversity – Friendly Local Self Government" "A Lobby note for integration of LGBTIQ Rights and Demands into the Local Self Governance Framework in Kerala." Centre for Development Studies. 2017. Thiruvananthapuram.

3

Transgenders- A Journey of a Thousand Miles

— Dr. Mohan Varughese and Krupa Susan Varghese

"Samaani va Aakootihi Samaanaa Hridayaanivah, Samaanamastu vo Mano Yathaa Vah Susahaasati ("Let there be oneness in your resolutions, hearts and minds; let the determination to live with mutual cooperation be firm in you all")". – RigVeda, Mandala-5, Sukta-60, Mantra-5

Transgenders, a colloquial term used to denote people who have a different identity than the others who claim to be a normal human with correct genetic design. Identity can be defined as a psychological move to know the truth about one's own self. It can vary from person to person according to time and needs of the era. Time is a shaper of everything; it makes history and creates future.

Human beings have evolved through various stages and reached a phase where nothing much needs to be changed. Evolution has completed the species' fight for survival. But for some it still remains a question when it comes to their biological difference which makes them deprived in the society where commonalities are celebrated.

This stigma in the minds have built a society where uniqueness is seen as a curse to the society's ethical values. Throughout history this curse has haunted the Great Indian Empires. Although, the service of transgenders was utilised by these empires, the royal gestures never brought them the acceptance or identity of their race. They were termed in different names- Hijras, Eunuchs, Aravani and Shiv- Shakti – the identities never cherished by the transgenders.[1]

The work of transgenders was greatly appreciated and being loyal to the royal was the norm. Keeper of the bed, protector of women quarters and the supplier of information through espionage were duties assigned to them which they performed to royal satisfaction. Besides, there is a mention about them in Kama Sutra (a Hindu text). Moreover, there has been a significant role played by them as per the description in important texts of Hinduism like *The Mahabharata and The Ramayana.*[2]

Mythological perspective created a distinctive twist to the transgender identity by framing a concept called 'Ardhanarishwara' (synchronising the masculine and feminine energies of the universe- Purusha and Prakriti) followed by the illustration of Shakti (the female principle of God) and Shiva (the male principle of God) a unity which is the progenitor of all creations.[3]

Pride during Mughal days

Members of transgender community held various positions in the administration during the Mughal era in India. It surprised many foreign merchants during their visit to India when they witnessed the power and prestige enjoyed by the transgender community in the imperial household.[4] These celebrated positions they enjoyed were included in the accounts of foreign historians and travellers.

During the Mughal era, it was a cake walk for them in establishing their rights. But the advent of British rule changed the flow of water upward which made the going tough for them. The empire where 'sun never sets' reintroduced darkness into the lives of transgenders. These people who are never accepted by the family or society are forced to lead orphan lives. Although they laid down their lives for the royal household, their efforts were in absolute vain.

Scholars like Shaun Marmon in her book '*Eunuchs and sacred boundaries in Islamic society*' noted the British traveller Eldon Rutter's reaction when he saw the presence of eunuch guards in Medina in 1925.[5] The reason behind such commitment displayed by the transgenders is due to their sacred relationship with the Prophet. It has been said that they are employed to vigil upon the women masquerading as devotees at Mataf, violating the norms.

Oppression under the British Raj

The introduction of 1871 Criminal Tribes Act (CTA) marked the beginning of their plight. The Act insisted upon registration and control of the third-genders. Under this, wearing female clothes was made a punishable offence for men and dancing or playing music was declared as violation of law. Such gestures would be punishable with two years of imprisonment and fine. This legislation brought by the British was discriminatory as it deprived transgenders of their basic rights and source of income. This pushed them to the edge of the society and they were banished to live a life marked by unequal treatment and complete oblivion.

The Englishmen created a new identity for these people during the British Raj in India. The LGBTQ segment of Indian population was treated as a distinct group with a unique socio-cultural identity. This classification resulted in further marginalisation of the transgenders who were completely cut off from all existing social norms. British response towards them inculcated a new outlook among all the religious leaders considering transgenders as a dirty and vulgar race.[6] The going became tougher for transgenders as societal acceptance was confined to two sexes - male and female, which the Indian society followed religiously. Homosexuality was portrayed as unethical and illegal. Despite Britishers wanting to erase the very existence of transgender identity, their efforts did not succeed completely. Nevertheless, many religious leaders still follow the same paths their colonial masters created.

Post - Independence Existence

During the Prime Ministership of Jawaharlal Nehru, the Criminal Tribes Act of 1871 was repealed as it was considered a hurdle to the description of 'free India'. But the spirit of this Act was not repealed completely. In 1957, the Government of Independent India passed a fresh Act named 'Habitual Offenders Act', incorporating the essence of the CTA of 1871.[7]

A number of amendments were brought to remove the anomalies and discrepancies in the aforesaid Act. But all the efforts of the Government of India to improve the social status of transgenders were futile as the stigma regarding them had already penetrated deep into the blood of Indians. Rights guaranteed by the Constitution of India also appears to be discriminatory when it comes to giving justice to a transgender. The 'just' society looks with suspicion when it is the transgender on the other side of the spectrum. The year 2008 witnessed a demand from the transgender community to revive the social welfare benefits which they enjoyed during the Mughal era. Subsequently they are allowed to fill up application forms for various purposes bearing columns indicating genders beyond male and female as other category. Now debates are on in the issue of allowing legal sanctity to transgender marriages. Also, transgenders are beginning to be productively employed in careers by various agencies. When Cochin Metro Rail Project was launched in the year 2017, the loco pilots were chosen from among LGBTQ community. Today seats are reserved for transgenders in educational institutions and are receiving dignified treatment in public places in addition to school and college campuses. This is a quantum jump from the inhumane treatment during the bygone era.

False Hope in the Era of Justice?

21st century is considered as an era of human rights along with the rights of different sexes. The Norwegian statement, 2006 recognised wide-scale violations of human rights based on sexual orientation and gender identity on behalf of 54 states at the UN Human Rights Council.[8] It urged the Council for a special session to discuss these issues as a first step towards addressing these violations. The International Commission of Jurist and the International Service for Human Rights, on behalf of a group of human rights organisation developed the Yogyakarta principles. The principle was named such because it was developed at Yogyakarta, Indonesia, to establish certain legal promises to affirm the role of states to protect the rights of all human beings irrespective of any sexual orientation.[9]

The judgements related to transgenders' rights are very crucial to India. The long-awaited acknowledgment of the transgender identity came to fruition in 2009 when the Government of India through the Election Commission provided voter identity cards to transgenders marking their gender as the third-gender. Later under the landmark judgement named NALSA, the Supreme Court of India titled them with the status of third gender. This judgement gave them right to protect their rights under the constitution and laws formed by state legislatures and parliament. The crux of the whole judgement is laid down in the words of Justice K S Radhakrishnan who stated that "recognition of transgenders as a third gender is not a social or medical issue but a human rights issue" (BBC News 2014). The Judgement awards them all rights under the constitution of India.[10]

They are smashed out from their homes in their small ages because of their sexual orientation. They are deprived of family and social support at a very young age. Access to education, health services and appearances in public places are viewed with suspicion by the society.

In India, Tamil Nadu is the only state which focus on introducing welfare programmes for Aravani (locally called). The setting up of telephone helpline called "Manasu" is a logical step in the formation of India's first helpline for the LGBTQIA (Lesbian, Gay, Bisexual, Transgender, Queer, Intersex, Asexual) community at Madurai in 2011.

The state of Kerala became the first state to showcase the rights of transgenders through the adoption of transgender policy against discrimination of transgenders. The policy shed light into the creation of Transgender Justice Board with Social Justice Minister of State as its chairperson. There were free sex reassignment surgeries too for them.

The Section 377 of the Indian Penal Code, 2018 came as a package of relief for them. It proclaimed the legal right to live with dignity. The government introduced several schemes to ensure employment opportunities for them which opened up new clouds in the sky where they can shine as rainbows forever.

Does these rights offer them a place in society? Will it create an end to their miseries? Is it a beginning of prosperous times for them? All these questions are difficult to decipher because in literal terms the schemes remain in the documents and the implementation is a hard reality. These rights never rescued them in the time of necessity. It has always been twisted to suit the preconceived notions and vested interest of the society dominated by 'normal people'. The stigma remains which has to be changed through proper adaption and implementation of governmental schemes and programmes.

Justice Prevailed or Denied?

Even in the midst of all the laws in favour of them this community live the life of lust and ignorance. The major justification for this statement is laid in the backyards of the red streets which push them into the dark rooms of flesh trade.

India being a conservative society has witnessed the cruel testimonies of rape. The country is ranked as one of the dangerous places for a woman. There has been a continuous debate and protest against sexual violence. But all these big talks are buried and transgenders demands swept under the carpet when it comes to equality and dignified treatment in society. This marks the statement more approachable 'justice delayed is justice denied'. In the same way when a transgender woman is raped, all fingers are pointed towards her because the stigma of suspicion is still prevailing in the society.

The society forces them to take up certain jobs like prostitution which even curtails their freedom as a citizen. They are forced by the pressures of the society which makes them submit to such coercion. Freedom for them is a lost dream which finds reference during the Mughal era. The attitude of the society opens the pandora's box before them.

Does poverty make them walk the paths of prostitution? Should the attitude of the society be blamed? The answer lies in the question. The nature of the society pushes them dwell in poverty. They choose it not as a means to satisfy their sexual needs but due to extreme psychological coercion. Privilege of choice is not for them; it is call of hunger which draws them to tread the path of prostitution.

Conclusion

Even when all schemes are professed there are dim lights in the system which give opportunity to transgender but rarely fulfil it. The system makes them corrupt and later blames them for corrupting the system and spoiling the ethical values. The question of good breed and bad breed also takes place under this banner of discussion.[11]

It would be more 'ethical' for the normative society which uphold norms and values to address them as Harijans (The People of God), a connotation which Mahatma Gandhi used for attributing to the discriminated sections of the society. A better approach and empathy to fellow beings makes the true essence of life in this world. Peace is not to preach; it is to practice among homo sapiens.

References

1. Aarefa Johari, "Hijra, kothi, aravani: a quick guide to transgender terminology", see website https://scroll.in/article/662023/hijra-kothi-aravani-a-quick-guide-to-transgender-terminology, accessed on 2 November 2019.
2. "A Brief History of Hijra, India's Third Gender", *'Culture Trip'*, see website https://theculturetrip.com/asia/india/articles/a-brief-history-of-hijra-indias-third-gender/, accessed on 2 November 2019.
3. Sadhguru, "Ardhanarishvara – When the Ultimate Man Became Half-Woman" (Isha: India, Jun 23, 2014), see website https://isha.sadhguru.org/in/en/wisdom/article/ardhanarishvara, accessed on 2 November 2019.
4. Adrija Roychowdhury, "When eunuchs were the mid-rung of power in the Mughal empire", see website https://indianexpress.com/article/research/eunuch-security-guards-bihar-mughal-empire-history-5266102/, accessed on 2 November 2019.
5. Adrija Roychowdhury, "When eunuchs were the mid-rung of power in the Mughal empire", '*The Indian Express*', 19 July, 2018, see website https://

indianexpress.com/article/research/eunuch-security-guards-bihar-mughal-empire-history-5266102/, accessed on 2 November.

6. Progya Ghatak, "Etched in our minds: The Criminal Tribes Act 1871", see website https://www.forwardpress.in/2015/03/etched-in-our-minds-the-criminal-tribes-act-1871/, accessed on 2 November 2019.
7. Dona John, "Living a Life of Exclusion Being a Transgender in Modern India", see website https://fnst.org/sites/default/files/uploads/2017/11/20/focuahumanrights-rightsoftransgenderinindia-donajohn.pdf, accessed on 2 November 2019.
8. Mousumi Padhi and Purnima Anjali Mohanty, "Securing Transgender Rights through Capability Development", *'Economic and Political Weekly'*, Vol. 54, Issue No. 1, 05 Jan, 2019, see website https://www.epw.in/engage/article/securing-transgender-rights-education-finance, accessed on 2 November 2019
9. *Ibid.*
10. *Ibid.*
11. "Section 377: Here is everything you need to know", *The Economic Times,* see website https://economictimes.indiatimes.com/news/politics-and-nation/sc-delivers-historic-verdict-heres-everything-you-need-to-know-about-section-377/articleshow/65698429.cms, accessed on 2 November 2019.

4

State, Law and Sexuality: An Examination of Sexuality in India with Special Reference to Section 377

— Sunil Mohan

Introduction

As a colonised nation for two centuries, modern India's conjectures of sexual relations and the idea of sexuality have been influenced by a complex mixture of colonial values, enlightenment knowledge and missionary morality. As various studies on Europe's encounter with India has showed, the land of India had once been an exotic object in the European imagination. Everything here fantasised the European mind and they approached India as a land of mysterious sexual relations, lucid morality and civilisational imperfection. As various scholars have pointed out, two century long colonisation has its implications in India at two levels. Firstly, colonial value system and the diffusion of modernity transformed the existing practices of social relationship in India. Secondly, we are not in a position to argue that ancient India had a peculiar system of sexuality as it a mixture of various practices, customs and reflections of social reality and imagination. Therefore, any debate on the role of sexuality or sexual relationships or gender in India has to be problematised within the ambit of plurality and colonial responses. With these ideas, this paper tries to problematise the issue of sexuality in India context with special reference to Section 377 of India Penal Code. As we would agree, the Indian Penal Code of 1861 has been, more or less, an invention of British intelligentsia to regulate the life and society in the colonised India. As Europeans, including the British, have imagined their culture as the supreme culture, they paid absolutely little attention to the systems and customs of indigenous society. Instead of looking at these systems of cultures as organic and open systems, in the British imagination they represented nothing but obscurantism. It was natural for the British mind to institute legal formalities to 'civilise' what they thought as uncivilised in India. Here comes the effort to open the debate of natural and unnatural dichotomy in sexuality in Indian contexts.

One may note that 6th September 2018 has been celebrated in the national media and other social platforms as a historic day. The celebration of this day can be seen as a part of the victory of modern Indian systems of thought over the traditional and colonial mentality of British legal system. The importance of this day can be traced back to a judgement by the apex court of India. On this day, through an epic judgement the Supreme Court of India had scrapped the colonial legal maxim contained under Section. 377 of Indian Penal Code. By scrapping Section 377 of IPC the Indian judicial system changed the conceptual perspectives on ethics and morality associated with sexuality and sexual orientations. The Supreme Court verdict scrapping Section 377, active in India since 1860, can be seen as an open declaration that the Indians and their culture need not be measured on the basis of colonial jurisprudence. Moreover, it shows that Indian judiciary wants to free India's legal framework from the clutches of colonial laws. It is said that legislation and codes of law are intertwined with a country's social values and cultural vibrancy. It can also be argued that only through upholding the philosophical systems of India the judicial-political analysis of Section 377 will be meaningful to the contemporary readers. This paper is intended to examine the imposition of Section 377 and subsequent legal frameworks on sexual identity in Indian Context. Such an attempt is necessary because colonial interventions in the field of Indian legal consciousness have replaced ancient India's plural forms of legal norms. Instead, this paper shows that legal frameworks have established a monolithic pattern of legal framework in the country.

India's Past and Sexuality

A survey of literature can show that Indian mythology provides the most liberal instances of homosexuality and that the landscape had accepted and accommodated many forms of eroticism within its culture, including homo eroticism. The country's long and troubled past reveals a gradual descent into Puritanism and homophobia due to caste consciousness and foreign religious influence. There is a general perception that homosexuality reached the soil of India through medieval West Asia and the intervention of modern

European cultural thought. Even though the historicity of this argument is not known, we may note that serious examination of the roots of homosexuality in Indian society is necessary.

From ancient period onwards Indians had a well-knitted sense on sexuality and sexual orientations. Vatsyana's '*kamasutra*' is the finest example, and apart from this almost every Indian literature and scriptures have themes related to sexual relations. In this paper the question of how Indian society and various sources considered or viewed homosexuality prior to the advent of foreign domination is examined. If we begin with ancient Indian mythology, it put on the idea that sexuality is a natural act involving romance and love between men and women for procreation and happiness. However, a sharp demarcation can be seen in the case of homosexuality as procreation is not possible. *Srimad Bagavatha* describes that Lord *Brahma* had created some demons obsessed with sex who wants to have sex with the creator himself. Seeing this, Lord Brahma got frightened and ran away. This story proves that the act of homosexuality has been frequently appeared in ancient Indian social consciousness.

All sources which help in reconstructing the ancient Indian social conditions gave a detailed description about the presence of various sexual groups and their condition in Indian social systems. For example, *Mahabharatha* gives numerous examples of same sex attachments. Similarly, Bengali Ramayana written by *Kritivasa*, the birth of sage *Bhagiratha* is ascribed to the sexual reunion between two females. *Matsyapurana,* contains the story of *Ila* and the concept Hari-Hara, the *Rig Veda* says '*vikrithievamprakrithi*' means diversity is what nature is all about and also quoted that homosexuality is said to have existed since the dawn of creation. In *kamasutra*, homosexuality is permissible to some communities and forbidden to others. Even homosexual copulation is represented in scriptures, carvings, paintings and icons of ancient India. The two texts which condemned homosexuality are *Manusmriti* and *Naradasmriti.*

References to homosexuality can be found not in the ancient texts, Vedas, sutras, puranas, legends but also in the Buddhist and Jain religious texts of the 6th century B.C. For example, *Puggalappasadasu Dutta* and *Anguttara Nikaya* contain warning against homoerotic desire, *Vinaya* is like that of a catalogue on various sexual dysfunctions ascribed to *pandaka*, compared to present day impotence and homosexuality. *Abhidarmasamuccaya* mentions men as forbidden sexual objects for other men. According to certain other Buddhist sources, the people belong to third genders were prohibited from learning, preaching and even giving donations to monks and nuns. Above mentioned aspect raise a question that how a society, which had a broad view that sexuality was really two persons privacy, would eventually get into a legal context. Section 377 of the Indian Penal Code is a reminder of the Victorian ethics enacted by the biblical canonical laws.

Colonial Law in India

The establishment of East India Company's rule in India also created space for the institutionalisation of legal practices in the country. In the British imagination, Indian law was characterised by a set of traditional systems and concepts. These 'outdated concepts', British scholars in India argued would not go hand-in-hand with the modern forms of legal practices. Therefore, the effort was to modernise and westernise the Indian legal systems. In a recent study, Aziz Rahman, Mohsin Ali, Saad Kahn have argued that "the British codified laws in India in terms of the rationalisation of law in the Weberian sense to ensure "order," "certainty" and "uniformity" (DeSousa, 2008, p. 68), as well as Bentham's liberal ideas of the rule of law and equality principles (Kolsky, 2010). These laws,while giving a sense of uniformity to the rule of law, were also used against the local populace to suppress uprisings".[1] The efforts to legalise and westernise the Indian legal practices were performed at two different levels. On the one hand, the colonial authorities have extensively searched the law books/legal codes/ authentic legal maxims in India. This search, prompted by the European standards, resulted in the invention of various legal texts such as the *manusmriti* and *dharmashastras*. British scholars soon recognised these texts as authentic legal texts in India and represented the faults of these texts as the faults of Indian legal systems. For example, 'Under so called Hindu law, a Brahmin murderer might not be put to death, while a *Sudra* who cohabited with a high-caste woman would automatically suffer execution. Under the new law, Brahmin and *Sudra* were liable to the same punishment for the same offence'[2]. Such kinds of codes were considered as legal texts and colonial authorities presumed that they were followed word-to-word in India. On the other hand, colonial authorities recognised that India did not have a state-centred legal system as in the West. The laxity of India in producing a state-centred legal system was read as an example for lawlessness in the country. The suggested remedy was to establish state-centred and punishment-oriented regulations in the form of law. This was natural as law for the colonial mind was a set of codes or regulations placed upon society and individuals. To the western legal concepts, these regulations were to be strictly adhered to and any violations would have resulted in punishments.

In 1860, the imperial rule introduced the first anti-sodomy law in India forbidding sexual intercourse between same sexes. But the law, which was introduced in India, was different from what it was in England, and it had a legal system that exempted homosexuals from being punished. This double stand shows the discriminatory nature of the British legal maxim which would treat people on their physical difference.

> "Whoever voluntarily has carnal intercourse against the order of nature with any man, woman or animal, shall be punished with imprisonment for life, or with imprisonment of either description for a term, which may extended to ten years, and shall be liable to fine"[3]

One needs to note down the usages like 'order of nature', 'animal' to understand that European imagination of sexuality had been undergoing a very turbulent era of transformation. What made this turbulent era of transformations is the extension of colonialism to far off places like that of India and Africa. The establishment of colonial systems in these areas made it compulsory that the British people were forced to experience and witness the lucid forms of sexual orientations practised in these areas. This meant to produce cultural shocks to the British minds as they were not equipped to normalise the plural sexual practices of these colonises.

Moreover, social subjugation in the colonies demanded an ideological subjugation. It was argued that by projecting Indians or other colonised as demoralised groups, colonialism could make justifications for its own inhuman activities. While the ideological presumptions of colonial rule in India was modelled on demoralising the Indian customs and practises, the implementation of Section 377 also indicates the move towards instituting formal legal structures. By implementing the Section 377, colonial authorities wanted to establish the fact that legal systems in India needed to be modernised and that the existing practices and customs were outdated. It was in these circumstances that the efforts to formalise the Indian legal systems began.

Conclusions

As we noted, the establishment of colonial legal practices India marks towards the beginning of formalised, state-oriented and institutionalised form of law making in the country. Instead of the various plural forms of legal practices and customs, the establishment of formal law making bodies and their efforts to propagate the diffusion of formal law in the country opened the doors for colonial making programme. Law, whether on sex or on property, has been replaced with notions of state, formality and a set of procedures. It was in this context that we see the beginning of formal courts of law in the country. The establishment of formal legal structures opened the debate of normal-abnormal practices and sex or sexual practices invited wide attention in the nineteenth century.

Homosexuality, lesbianism or other forms of sexual practices are not new to India. Being one of the oldest and plural civilisations in the world, Indian civilisations had various currents of social practices and bodily forms. Indian civilisations were never been subject to homogenous practices. We need to emphasise that India had produced one of the most authentic forms of sexual knowledge in the form of *Vatsyayana's Kamasutra*, a treatise of sexuality. Further, various carvings in ancient and mediaeval India temples and numerous literary works demonstrate the plural forms of sexual practices in the various civilisations in the country. Section 377 of Indian Penal Code can be seen as part of a large debate to formalise and modernise the multitude of sexual relations and practices in India. In this sense, Section 377 represents nothing but colonial jurisprudence coupled with elite-centred attempts to establish monolithic sexual culture in India.

Notes

1. Volume 25 Number 1. Decolonizing Through a Peace and Conflict Studies Lens.
2. The Economic and Social Impact of Colonial Rule in India Chapter 3 of Class Structure and Economic Growth: India & Pakistan since the Moghuls Maddison (1971), p. 4.
3. The Indian Penal Code (Act XLV of 1860): With Notes.

References

1. Merchant, Hoshang. 'Indian Homosexuality: Ancient India to Contemporary India', Allied Publishers, 2010.
2. Vanita, R., Kidwa, S. 'Same-Sex Love in India: Readings in Indian Literature', Palgrave, New York, 2001.
3. Wilhelm, Amara Das. 'Tritiya-Prakriti: People of the Third Sex: Understanding Homosexuality, Transgender Identity and Intersex Conditions Through Hinduism, Xlibris Corporation, 2010.
4. Doniger, Wendy. 'Redeeming the Kamasutra', Oxford University Press, 2016.
5. Keen, Karen R. 'Scripture, Ethics, and the Possibility of Same-Sex Relationships', Wm. B. Eerdmans Publishing, Michigan, 2018.
6. Han, Enze, O'Mahoney, Joseph. 'British Colonialism and the Criminalisation of Homosexuality: Queens, Crime and Empire', Routledge, 2018.

7. Peterson, Neil, Brian. 'What was the Sin of Sodom: Homosexuality, Inhospitality, or Something Else?', Wipf and Stock Publisher, USA, 2016.
8. Agarwal, K. Manjul. 'From Bharata to India: Volume 2: the Rape of Chrysee', iUniverse, Inc., Bloomington, 2012.
9. Doniger, Wendy. ' The Hindus: An Alternative History', Oxford University Press, New York, 2009.
10. Gupta, Alok. 'This alien legacy: the origins of "sodomy" laws in British colonialism', Human Rights Watch Publisher, 2008.
11. Aldrich, Robert. 'Colonialism and Homosexuality', Routledge, 2008.
12. Naik, Yeshwant. 'Homosexuality in the Jurisprudence of the Supreme Court of India', Springer, 2107.
13. Fraser, Robert. 'Book History Through Postcolonial Eyes: Rewriting the Script', Routledge, 2008.

5

Empowering Transgenders through Entrepreneurship

— Nayana, BS

We proudly say India is a country where unity in diversity exists. We live in a diverse community, representing all religious, ethnic, racial and social backgrounds. Transgenders are also one of the elements in that diversity. The number of transgenders is increasing rapidly in the society. The reason for this is because of the awareness in society regarding identifying the broad transgender spectrum. Eventhough, the visibility of transgender people is increasing in popular culture; we still face severe discrimination, stigma and systemic inequality. There are many transgender people, who compromised their identity for satisfying their social needs. Despite of their gender dysphoria, they were forced to get married or lead a so called "normal" family life. The major reason for this was the fear of society, fearing they would lose the social relations and family members because of their gender disclosure. Shakunthala Devi, an Indian writer popularly known as the "human computer" was one of the victims of such compromised marriage life. Her husband was a gay and she knew it very lately. It was a deep shock, but later she made genuine efforts to study the plights of homosexual community in India and documented her experiences too.

The word "transgender" – or trans – is an umbrella term for people whose gender identity is different from the sex assigned to us at birth. The word "transgender" and it's modern definitions of it only came into use in the late 20th century. In a democratic country like India, we have the right to choose or deny a religion despite of in which we are born. Likewise, gender is also a personal choice and sex is not the criteria to determine the gender. Gender identity is your internal sense of whether you are male or female.The struggle for acceptance, protection and visibility for transgenders is still continuing. There are many transgenders who are the living examples who made their success story through their achievements. Sathyasri Sharmila (lawyer), Joita Mondal (Judge), Prithika Yashini (Police officer), Shabnam Mausin (MLA) are some among them. Empowering the transgender community is a biggest task. For empowerment, self-occupation is a proven model.

Entrepreneurship is one such self occupation. Entrepreneurship is the process of setting up a business, running it successfully by expecting a profit on their investment. The people who create these businesses are called entrepreneurs. Entrepreneurs are considered as national assets to be cultivated, nurtured, and motivated to the greatest possible extent. Great entrepreneurs have the ability to change the way we live and work. With their successful innovations, they improve the standards of living. Also, in addition to creating wealth with entrepreneurial ventures, they also create jobs and contribute to a growing economy.

Transgenders and entrepreneurship

Social acceptance and inclusion are the major areas to be addressed in the transgender community. The degree of risk in transgenders' journey of life starts from the very basis. To be very specific, when every individual after a point of time looks for the future career and prospects of life, it is at this moment that these people are in real search of their own gender identity to understand who they are. Having isolated from family, social stigma, school dropouts, illiterate, unemployed, poverty, prone to physical abuse, homelessness, health hazards, invalid credentials, arrest on false allegations, psychological trauma and attempt to suicides are the major issues or challenges faced by this community. Entrepreneurship is a skill. It does not demand an educational degree to get through it. Entrepreneurial spirit leads an individual to achieve success in the form of profit and goodwill in their business career. Entrepreneurial spirit is characterised by innovation and risk-taking. Entrepreneurship can offer levels of fulfillment and achievement to an individual. For a marginalised community, staying together for existence is very important. Entrepreneurship is a gateway for such community to grow up. "She roses Hangouts" is one of the best examples to exhibit as an initiative whose entrepreneurial spirit is possessed. It is a cafeteria run by acid attack victims for providing employment and emotional support to women survivors of acid attacks. They are actively engaged in social work not only by providing employment to the victims, but also by donating their profits to International Foundation for Crime Prevention.

This successful business model can be adopted by transgenders for finding their livelihood. Beauty industry is one of the major field where the interest of the transgenders are vested with. We have many makeup artists and fashion designers from the transgender community. This interest should be nurtured by injecting the entrepreneurial spirit for building an enterprise using their skill and talent. When they involve themselves in socially accepted business activities with social consciousness the society will be ready to accept them. They should take all efforts to utilise concessions extended by the government and empathy of the society. When their attitude and behaviour earn the confidence of banks they will readily come forward to fulfill their financial requirements. Entrepreneurial orientation on analytical and decision-making skills has to be enhanced regularly which may help in overcoming the fear of imitativeness and promote their social status. Transgender entrepreneurs should have their autonomous SHGs and NGO Advisory Councils so that there is all time mobility of funds and can help in boosting more entrepreneurship among transgenders.

Proper credentials and platforms should be given so that they can avail the amenities for infrastructure like allocation of land, transportation, water, electricity etc. to establish the location of business. Bureaucracies norms can be liberalised exclusively for them so that they can be registered under DIC. There are several Entrepreneur Development Programmes conducted in state levels and national levels. Several workshops are also conducted for enhancing the entrepreneurship in the economy. These programmes need to get circulated in the transgender society for motivating them to be an entrepreneur. Being financially independent can solve their problems to a greater extend. They can get eliminated from begging, prostitutions and drug addictions. Live and Let Live should be the phenomenon of humanity and trans community is now slowly being viewed in a new light and has a vivid prosperous growth of entrepreneurship with well advancement of technology and other innovative movements which benefit the entrepreneurs, transgender community, society and the whole of the nation.

References

- Singh, Sheobalal (1985). "Entrepreneurship and Social Change", Rawat Publications, Jaipur.
- Patel, V.D. (1987). Entrepreneurship Development Programmes in India: It Reflection for Developing Countries, Ahmadabad, Entrepreneurship Development Institute of India.
- Suguna, M (2013). Self help groups a panacea for the socio-economic development of transgenders in Tamil Nadu. Periyar University.

6

Gender and Sexual Minorities in Kerala: An Over View to Kerala's Gender Sensitive Initiatives Towards Them

— Lijitha

Abstract

Gender and sex, to this date, are concepts many people don't comprehend. They either choose to ignore these ideas or just completely reject them. For centuries gender has defined, shaped and limited the role of individual in the society. The law as well as religious fundamentalists is trying to oppress LGBTIQ person's visibility all over the world, particularly in India. They are still struggling to claim an identity. But Kerala being a trailblazer, from being the first Indian state to achieve 100 percent primary education to controlling the population growth rate, and making it the lowest among all Indian states in the last ten years, its stand towards sexual minorities is quite impressive. The unique policies formulated in Kerala have made things a lot easier for them. This particular article tries to understand and vividly explain the visibility of sexual minorities in the state: especially the transgender section; and also tries to focus on the various policy made by the state for their inclusion in the main stream society.

Key words: *Sexual Minority, Transgender visibility in Kerala, social participation, Kerala transgender policy.*

Introduction

Most of the states have one or more minority groups within their national territories characterised by their own identities, which differ from that of the majority population. The LGBTIQ[1] community, undoubtedly, is the most prominent among highly-marginalised social groups in Kerala which have recently shed the mantle of darkness and gained visibility; are the gender and sexual minorities. They have faced violence and humiliation across many centuries; still prevent them from living open lives. In recent times it appears clear that they are not small in number, many of them are coming out of the veil and openly disclosing and discussing their sexuality and gender. Even though most members of this community are suppressed and denied their rights, a small section of this community have gained legal recognition. Following the Supreme Court's ruling to affirm the transgender community's freedom from discrimination and right to equality in 2014, Kerala became the first state to introduce a transgender policy in 2015. The 'State Policy for Transgender in Kerala 2015' provisions to protect the community by providing equal access to social and economic resources, protecting the right to equal treatment under the law, the right to life, liberty and justice, and the right to non-discrimination based on sex. It also includes a plethora of progressive steps for the recognition, inclusion, and empowerment of the community, including Transmen, Transwomen, and intersex individuals in economic and social opportunities, public transport, health, social security, education, and career sectors; thus is setting a strong example across India and abroad.

In India, there is a plural and diverse transgender population which is spread across the country. Based on the geographical area they have to know the different name in different place such as Hijras, Aravanis, Tirunangais, Kothis, Jogtas and Jogappas, Shiv Shaktis, Kinnars[2], etc. They are most among the vulnerable and marginalised population. Transgenders have faced great adversities from their childhood; experience a poor quality of life that continues well into their adulthood. Before the Kerala's renowned transgender policy, their life in this state was also not much different. Exclusion from mainstream, social stigma and zero visibility was very much there. Since the Supreme Court's ruling their lives have changed and also their hopes and apprehensions for the future. Here Kerala as a state is trying to be a role model for the rest of the country and to the world through its inclusive policies and attitude towards this community.

Understanding the LGBTIQ: the Gender and Sexual Minorities

LGBTIQ persons are gender and sexual minorities. Generally sexual minority denotes the whole LGBTIQ community but it is a misconception. Lesbian, gay, bisexual and asexual (LGBA) are the sexual minorities. Intersex and Transgender (I&T) people are gender minorities. The gender and sexual minorities are the people who got discriminated due to their sexual identity/orientation or gender identity. This includes lesbians, gays, bisexual, transgenders, intersex and queer person's etc... Queer is an umbrella term to denote all sexual minorities. It refers to a population of people united by having gender identities or sexual orientations that differ from the heterosexual majority. Other names for this population include GSM (Gender and Sexuality Minorities), GSD (Gender and Sexuality Diverse).

It is essential to understand the concept of identities such as gender and sex as a continuum to know how transgender realise their identity. Sex of a person is assigned to them at birth based on visual assessment of baby's genital presentation[3]. Sex is also on a continuum as there are 40 different intersex conditions out of which only one-third is visible to naked eye according to the Intersex Society of North America[4]. Unger (1979) defines gender as a "term used to describe the non-physiological components of sex that are culturally regarded as appropriate to males or females"[5]. Gender is an identity that has been carefully constituted in time that is established through a specifically styled repetition of acts[6]. Gender is an emotional state and hence, there is no 'real' or 'true' gender, it is what we experience ourselves to have [7]. Gender expression, which is the outward expression of gender, cannot be confined in the binaries of masculine and feminine; it is rather a continuum and shifts shape over the course of one's lifetime[8]. The gender expressed is independent of their sex. Some people experience their sexual orientation and/or gender identity as fluid. This means that their identities might shift over time. Many other people experience their sexual orientation or gender identity as stable and enduring over time. This is also normal. Sexuality and gender are complicated, there are more variations and are the different shades in the rainbow.

Social Inclusion of Gender and Sexual Minorities in Kerala

After the 2009 Delhi High Court verdict, things are really looking promising in India and especially in Kerala. In Kerala, there are some positive initiatives to support LGBTIQ people both at governmental and non-governmental levels in the past few years. The Department of Social Justice (SJD) of the Government of Kerala, even before the Supreme Court decision, taken a progressive stance and initiated a survey to better understand the needs, priorities, and aspects of TGI social, economic and personal life. The survey estimated the presence of more than 25,000 TGIs in the state.

It was one of the first States in India to introduce a welfare policy for the transgender community in 2015. And later in 2016, introduced free Sex Reassignment Surgery (SRS) through government hospitals. As a part of its Transgender Policy, the government will introduce 'Gender Taxi' along the lines of 'She Taxi' which will be owned and operated by transgender people. Queer pride rallies also played a vital role in changing the mindset of Kerala's society.

Kannur, a District in Kerala in the year 2016 allocated a part of its budget towards the employment and skill training programmes for transgenders in Kerala. Thiruvananthapuram Corporation budget also allocated 20 lakhs of its present budget to the development of LGBTIQ people. Dr. Shashi Tharoor, Member of Parliament, is one of the strong proponents of LGBTIQ rights and introduced a private member's bill twice at the Lok Sabha for repulsion of Section 377 that criminalises sexual activity 'against the order of the nature'. Section 377 is widely misused by the police to harass LGBTIQ community members. In 2016, President Pranab Mukherjee also opened a 'Gender Park' in Kozhikode aimed at researching for policy with regards to the LGBTIQ community and its empowerment. The State Government has proposed several pilot initiatives to empower the group through this mechanism and is one of the first of its kind in India. Kerala has also empowered the transgender community with voting rights and strong social awareness and protection programmes. It also stood strongly against the discrimination of Transgenders in campuses.

The Malabar Cultural Forum based in Kozhikode has been conducting a state level cultural festival for transgenders "Orukam" for the last few years. Nileena Atholi, a young journalist at Mathrubhumi daily recently won the SBT Media Literary Award for her series on the lives of transgenders titled "Ardhajeevithangalude Arakshithavasthakal". Her aim was to give gender and sexual minorities visibility and spread awareness about their issues. She believes that artistic expression has direct impact on the lives of struggling communities and feels it is important for them to get many opportunities to prove their caliber and thereby enter the mainstream. Jayan Cherian's 'Ka-Bodyscapes' and Akhil Sathyan's 'That's my Boy', Avalilekkula Dooram (The Journey to Her) a documentary directed by P. Abhijith are the Malayalam films about the LGBTIQ lives. In the history of Malayalam press and literature, for the first time a queer column published in Mathrubhumi weekly. LGBTIQ activists and community members shared their life experiences and struggle in these articles.

Transgender Policy of Kerala Government 2015

The Honorable Supreme Court of India (vide judgment dated 15th April 2014) has firmly established the right to equality and equal protection for transgender persons under Article 14, 15, 16 by prohibiting discrimination on the ground of gender identity. It has expanded the scope of the term sex in Articles 15 and 16, which till recently referred only to binary genders of male and female, to include TG as a third gender.

The problems of TGs in India lies in the stigma and discrimination they have to face from the society, resulting in their exclusion from socio-political and economic spectrum. TGs have unique needs which are ignored by society. In view of the systematic injustices that prevent this minority community from realising equal rights and they are forced to live as second-class citizens in their own country. To rectify this situation State Government of Kerala issued the Transgender policy to ensure the constitutional rights of TGs, taking into account the Supreme Court judgment (2014) and the findings of the Kerala State TG survey. This policy covers all categories of TG including Male to Female TGs, Female to Male TGs and intersex people. The policy emphasises the rights of the citizens as man, woman or TG as stated in the judgment. This policy includes goals and objectives of TG policy, approaches, implementation process and selects areas of socio-economic development of TGs.

Policy Approaches

The basic approaches of the policy are the following:

- Ensure that all rights of TGs are protected and enforced, including the right to self-identification of gender as man, woman, TGs and the right to expression.
- Ensure equal access to all services of the Government.
- Support positive discrimination to address inequalities in areas of education, health, and public appointments.
- Raise public awareness of TG rights and develop capacity of relevant stakeholders to enforce rights.
- Provide proper mechanisms to ensure equal access to all services and benefits as well as effective mechanisms to address issues of violence and harassment faced by TGs.
- Effective implementation and monitoring that TG rights are being protected and implemented and fine tuning policy when required.

Goals and Objectives of TG Policy

The policy support the attainment of

- A just society where men, women and TGs have equal rights to access development opportunities, resources and benefits.

- The right to live with dignity and enjoy a life free from all forms of violence.
- The right to freedom of expression in all matters that affect them.
- Right to equal voice and participation in key development decisions that shape their lives, communities and the state.

Other Initiatives of Kerala to Support Gender Minorities

Other than transgender policy of Kerala state 2015, many more initiatives have been taken by the Kerala government for the empowerment of the sexual minorities of the state. States inclusive policies are:

- **Transgender Scholarship Scheme by Government of Kerala:**

  It is a huge boost and recognition for the transgender community, Syama a postgraduate has become the first transgender in Kerala to get an education scholarship of the Social Justice Department. It marks the beginning of the implementation apart of the Transgender Policy of Kerala 2015. "Gender education is limited to women. Sexual minorities and their problems are not discussed, in the class or in the curriculum. Only education can bring about change. Teachers too have to be aware of transgenders in their class and protect their interests". This is one of the reasons why Syama, who has done her MA in Malayalam from University College, wants to pursue her PhD in Education.

  Now, she has become the first recipient of the Rs 20,000 scholarship introduced by the state government as part of the transgender policy.

- **Sahaj International School:**

  Even though organisations like Kochi Metro are coming forward to provide job opportunity for transgenders, the lack of qualification is seen as a challenge among transgenders. To address this challenge the initiative like Sahaj International School came up. First time in India a residential transgender school named as 'Sahaj International School' was inaugurated in Kochi on December 30, 2016. The first batch of the residential school has 10 transgender students, who study under the National Open School system. Among the faculty members six transgender teachers were included and they are from the Trans India Foundation. In addition to make them to appearing in grade 10 and 12 board exams, the school will place focus on soft skill training, vocational training, personality development, organic farming, stitching etc. They focused on all-round development of skills among the community.

Famous transgender activist and artist Kalki Subramaniam inaugurated the school. The first batch of selected students came from different sections of the transgender community. The aim of a transgender school is to provide transgender security, salvation and sustainability. This initiative in Kerala has definitely lead transgenders to brighter road of education and employment.

The government has also issued orders giving two extra seats for transgenders in every course in universities and recognised arts and science colleges in the State.

- **Grant up to ₹ 2 lakhs to transgenders for sex reassignment surgery:**

  The Kerala State Government had introduced grant to transgenders for sex reassignment surgery. The grant up to ₹ 2 lakhs for the surgery. It implemented through the Social Justice Department. Kerala has assigned three hospitals for the gender reassignment surgery and it would also pay for people to undergo the procedure outside the state and reimburse those who had already done so. The initiative follows many of the steps that the Kerala Government has taken to improve the lives of transgenders. Governmental Medical Colleges in Kerala have laid out plans to have free-of-cost clinics opened exclusively for the transgender community, beginning at the Kottayam Medical College.

- **Manaswini: Kudumbashree Transgender Wing**

  As the part of empowering transgender people in Kerala Kudumbashree has launched it's first ever Ayalkoottam or Neighbourhood Group (NHG) for transgender community named 'Manaswini'. It has been registered under Kottayam Municipality North CDS as special NHG. Kudumbashree plans more such groups in the future with the participation of more people. The aim is to bring the members of the transgender community to the mainstream of the society.

- **IFFK 2016**

  The 21st International Film Festival of Kerala (IFFK, 2016), conducted by the Kerala State Chalachitra Academy offered special facilities to the transgender community including a

'Gender Bender Package.' A special category has been created for the registration of the transgender community for the first time. They also provided with a special toilet facility titled "We Toilet." The Gender Bender package includes a bunch of films, which has been appreciated by the lesbian, gay, bisexual, and transgender community around the world. This has section featured six films which propagate emotional, social, cultural and political situations of LGBTIQ society. This is for the first time IFFK shows its solidarity with the LGBTIQ community.

- **Queer Pride Keralam**

  Kerala celebrates its queer pride every year, the first time it was held at Thrissur on July 2nd in 2010. Queer pride is celebrated around the world by lesbian, gay, bisexual, transgender people and their supporters. Queer pride is a celebration. It is about loving who we are, whether lesbian, gay, bisexual, transgender, hijra or straight and affirming every one's rights to be respected. LGBTIQ people participated in the Pride to demand that they be treated as normal people. Activists of gender and sexual minority groups are hopeful that the event will improve awareness about them and get better acceptance.

- **CDS Triggers Sexual Minority Workplace Inclusion**

  Centre for Development Studies in Trivandrum has opened doors for employing a transgender person. Sree S. Sree who has been appointed as a Document Digitisation Assistant in CDS. Sree has a post graduate degree in Demography.

- **Indian Train Network Makes History by Employing Transgender Workers**

  An initiative offering jobs to members of Kerala's hijra community aims to tackle prejudice and bring transgender people into the mainstream. In an effort to integrate trans people into Indian society, Kochi's Metro has hired 23 members of the hijra community, all on contract through Kudumbashree, in different categories from ticket billing, customer-service to sanitation. Although some of them faced hiccups such as difficulties, finding accommodation and facing hostile/condescending behaviour from co-workers, most of them are now well-adjusted in their jobs. They used to beg on India's train network, but after this initiative, for the first time, transgender women have proper jobs, serving passengers and selling tickets in the south Indian city of Kochi.

Normally people don't interact with trans people. They live separately from society, they are not given jobs, and their rights are not respected. This initiative wanted to bring them into the mainstream by ensuring that people interact with them every day.

- **Transgender Athletic Meet**

  Kerala hosted an exclusive day-long transgender athletic meet, a first in the country, at the central stadium in the state capital on 28th April 2017.The event reflected the state's policy to stop the social stigma and ostracism that the transsexuals has been facing since British colonial times. The event has revealed fresh talents. Talent is generally suppressed in the community and this was an opportunity for them. The logo for the nation's first ever transgender athletics meet was released by veteran athlete Mercy Kuttan and around 200 persons from the community had participated from across the state.

- **Loans up to 3 lakh through KSWDC to start self-employment ventures**

  Government of Kerala has been decided to give a loan of up to 3 lakh to a transgender through the Kerala State Women's Development Corporation (KSWDC) to start self-employment ventures. Administrative sanction had been provided to hand over 30 lakh to the KSWDC for giving the loan to 10 persons. Training too had been given.

- **Wedding aid**

  Another initiative has been issued by the Government of Kerala to provide wedding assistance of 30,000 to transgender couples. The aid will be given if one of the partners is a transgender.

  All this programmes and supporting initiatives are the positive sign to empower the LGBTIQ community in Kerala. But the majority programmes and supporting ventures are mainly focused on the welfare of transgenders community. Other community members such as lesbian, gay, bisexual and intersex people are slightly disregarded. Another important fact is that Lesbians, gays and bisexuals remain marginalised due to laws in India, transgender people have secured legal rights in India. Government of Kerala has prepared a new bill to amend IPC 377 to decriminalise homosexuality in Kerala. Decriminalisation of homosexuality comes under the state list. The draft is pending for the approval of the authorities.

The road ahead

With many gender-sensitive projects in the pipeline, Kerala has plenty of plans to empower women and the transgender community in the upcoming years.

The Government of Kerala's department of Social Justice plans on increasing government capacity and efficiency in the Gender Park, a flagship initiative which "provides need-based capacity building and training to different groups, such as students, government officials and professionals, through specialised training modules on gender sensitivity, inclusion and awareness". As it is uniquely positioned to see through that recommendations are implemented by the government, the Gender Park has launched plans to commence off-campus activities focusing on the welfare of women and transgenders. There are also ideas to increase the size and capabilities of the research division in the International Institute for Gender and Development (IIGD) to "engage in solution-based knowledge management on different aspects of gender, development and governance."

The state capital, Thiruvananthapuram will soon have a model stretch "she-coridoor", wherein women can enjoy 'safety and women-friendliness' to the maximum. This road stretch will offer seating facilities, CCTV cameras, 'she-toilets', sanitary napkin vending machines, FM radio stations and other such beneficial facilities for women and the transgender comminity. The objective of the project is to turn the state capital a model women-friendly city, giving priority to their safety. Gender minorities should feel free and safe in the city. 2 crore rupees had been allocated for the same. The She-Coridoor stretch would also be a tribute to the valuable contributions made by women, featuring paintings and graphics of them from various fields including politics, arts, cinema, social activism etc…

Undoubtedly, Kerala is miles ahead of other Indian states in terms of gender-sensitive policies and thought processes. Initiatives and projects backed by governmental support are not only useful in changing the mindsets of people but also very important in paving the way to a gender equal society. It's time that other states take note and up their game too.

Notes

1. LGBTIQ- It's an acronym stands for Lesbian, Gay Bisexual, Transgender, Intersex and Questioning.
2. Ghosh, A. (2015). LGBTQ Activist Organisations as 'Respectably Queer' in India: Contesting a Western View. Gender, Work & Organisation.

3. Sennott, S., & Smith, T. (2011). Translating the sex and gender continuums in mental health: A transfeminist approach to client and clinician fears. Journal of Gay & Lesbian Mental Health, 15(2), 218-234
4. *Ibid.*
5. Unger, R. K. (1979). Toward a redefinition of sex and gender. American Psychologist, 34(11), 1085. (Butler, 1988)
6. Sennott, S., & Smith, T. (2011). Translating the sex and gender continuums in mental health: A transfeminist approach to client and clinician fears. Journal of Gay & Lesbian Mental Health, 15(2), 218-234
7. *Ibid,* p. 218.
8. The Hindu, Apr., 2017.

References

- High court of India: *NAZ Foundation v. government of NCT of Delhi and others*, 2009WP(C) No.7455/2001.
- Supreme Court of India. *Suresh Kumar Kaushal and another Appellants v. NAZ Foundation and Other respondents*, 2013 Civil Appeal No. 10974.
- Transgender policy of Kerala -2015, social justice department.
- A Ravathy (2010). *The Truth About Me -A Hijara Life Story*, Penguin Books India.
- 'Transgender Rights in India', The New York Times, April 25, 2014.
- Elizabeth Barnes (2016). *Valuing Disability, Causing Disability*, The University of Chicago Press.
- Surmail Singh (1999). 'Gender Dimension of Physical Disability', *Economic and Political Weekly.*
- Krishna, G. (2018, January). Transgenders in Kerala- Realisation of their Identity. (A. Paul, Ed.) *Journal of Social Work Education and Practice*, III(1).
- https://indianexpress.com/article/india/india-news-india/kerala-becomes-first-state-to-unveil-transgender-policy/
- https://timesofindia.indiatimes.com/city/thiruvananthapuram/here-comes-a-she-corridor-for-women-in-kerala/articleshow/63681224.cms
- http://www.newindianexpress.com/states/kerala/2017/aug/30/she-taxi-cabbies-in-kerala-drive-into-uncertainty-1649933.html
- https://genderpark.gov.in/shetaxi.html

7

Colonialism, Law and India's LGBTQ Community: A Historical Examination since 1860

— *Dr. R.S. Vineeth*

Introduction

Since 1947 India is a sovereign nation. Before being independent, India had experienced European colonisation leading to the nation's transition towards its contemporary position. Colonialism and colonial modernity are not without problems. Scholars across cultures and regions have pointed out at many times the issue of dominance and violence associated with colonialism.[1] The concept of structural violence is a viable model to examine the violence and terror associated with colonial institutions.[2] Every colonial institution used the method of force, violence, authority and surveillance to regulate the private and public life of the colonised. By and large, the use state's power to establish 'normalcy' in public and private life was quite common under colonialism. Through a chain of power and violence, colonialism created what the coloniser presented as normalcy in the colonies. In their attempt to breed regulated normalcy, colonial state replaced the existing patterns of social life, family, caste, individuality and language.[3] While colonial authorities redefined the nature of social/political/private/ public/ cultural systems in the colonies, the continuation of the legacies of colonialism during and after decolonisation is the natural sign of colonial mentality. Writing on colonialism, Frantz Fanon, the distinguished Algerian writer noted that;

> "Colonialism is not satisfied merely with holding a people in its grip and emptying the native's brain of all form and content. By a kind of perverted logic, it turns to the past of the people, and distorts, disfigures and destroys it"[4]

Fanon's psychological model provides an ample theory for analysing on colonialism. Fanon argues that the colonised continues to imbibe the cultural legacies of colonisers even after the eventual cessation of colonialism. Drawing on Fanon's theory, this article argues that colonial interventions in India, especially with regard to the perceptions on body and sexuality, resulted in two structural changes. On the one hand, colonial hegemony replaced Indian plural approaches towards sexuality with a uniform and state-centric approach. One needs to note that India had a history of multiple forms of sexual practices during the pre-colonial periods,[5] but sexuality in colonial India shows evidences of state-centric regularisation and institutionalisation of sexual life. On the other hand, the influence of colonial modernity continued to shape social consciousness of institutions/ culture in the post-colonial periods. This is evident if we recognise that after five decades of independence, India was reluctant to reconsider its policy towards Lesbian, Gay, Bisexual, Transgender and Queer (hereafter LGBTQQ) sections. Not only that successive Indian governments have failed to affirmatively recognise the legal existence of LGBTQs but colonial legal charters continues to shape India's official policies towards them. The lacuna in recognising LGBTQs in independent India's legal system is a direct reflection of colonial legacies on Indian society. We need to identify that this is where Fanon's arguments on colonialism that the psychology of colonial subordination continues in the veins and brains of colonies gains momentum in analyzing colonialism in India. Scholars have often pointed out that the epistemological form and structural edifice of India's legal framework are based on British legal system.[6] Colonial legal structure was based on the assumption that 'law is a body of rules that can be imposed on others by those who dominate the formal process of law-making'.[7] It goes without saying that colonial outlook characterised law in India as an authoritarian and dogmatic set of rules to be implemented upon subjects. It is very interesting to note that many intellectuals, especially Anglophilic Indians, were proud to accept that 'almost the entire legal system of India is today based on English Law'.[8] Banarjee, AC. 1984. English Law in India, New Delhi; Abhinav, p. 288. Reproduced in Werner Menski.

As we noted, two century long British colonialism replaced Indian legal systems with European legal framework. The colonial and western legal structure, providing 'legal modernity' in India, have failed to recognise the legal pluralism in Indian legal consciousness. The negation of legal pluralism transgender by colonial authorities can be seen as a part of colonial effort to introduce a positivist legal framework. What colonialism tried to introduce in India in the name of positivist legal framework was a form of state-centric authority. In this schema of state-centric positivist law, men to men and women- to women sexual relations along with transgender identity were looked at with suspicion. Subsequently, LGBTQs were regarded unnatural and as a deviation from normalcy. Instead of recognising the social reflections on LGBTQs in colonial India, colonial legal frameworks criminalised the so-called 'abnormal' sexualities and gender identities.[9] This new standardisation of sexual and gender pluralism was in direct opposition to the social and legal frameworks in pre-colonial India. As a consequence, transgender such as hijaras, eunuchs, kothis, aravanis, jogappas, shiv-shaktis were kept under state's watch and local authorities were given power to correct them.

In contemporary India, the dominant form of social consciousness tries to negate the existence of LGBTQs.This laxity in recognising the LGBTQ community comes from the hegemony of middle-class/upper-caste social consciousness in India. By social consciousness, this article indicates the value systems exercising authority on the cultural and social spheres of life. Since upper-caste/middle-class hegemony and male domination defines the purity/impurity discourse LGBTQs were regarded ugly and unlawful in popular imagination. On the contrary, survey of Indian literature indicates different sets of arguments. There are evidence to show that members of LGBTQs have been recognised in Indian mythologies and metaphysical literature. A close examination of Indian mythology shows that LGBTQs, especially transgender, are characterised not as people devoid of human virtues. Various Indian concepts of the divine is associated with one of the LGBTQ identities. Vedas, Puranas, Mahabharata and Ramayana recognise androgynous and hermaphroditic characters along with their ability to undergo sex-change. Stories of eunuchs, lesbians, bisexuals, homosexuals are often appear in ancient Indian literature which shows that Indian society had concerns over gender and sexual plurality.

Sexual and Gender Pluralism: Reflections from Past

Homosexual and transgender community is not a new phenomenon in India. Various ancient texts such as Manusmriti, Arthashastra, Kamasutra, Upanishad and Puranas deal with stories, legends or myths about homosexual relations.[10] The Concept of Tritiya Prakriti or Napumsaka is an integral part of Indian myths. The concept of Ardhanariswara is another classic example for sexual pluralism in Indian culture. As per the concept, god Shiva merges his consort goddess Parvathi to his body and creates a body of half male and half female. The concept of Ardhanariswara can be seen as the recognition of reality beyond the normalcy of biological identity.

Ardhanariswara shows that sexual union of male and female can produce human beings who are neither male nor female. Similarly, the union of god Vishnu and his consort Lekshmi produced the 'Lekshmi Narayana' representing gender plurality. Correspondingly, the Bahagavatha Purana gives the picture of Mohini, who is a beautiful woman form of the male god Vishnu. The Brahmanada Puranas shows that goddess Parvathi is ashamed to see her husband's effort to woo Mohini, the female form of god Vishnu. The concept of Ardhanariswara, Lekshmi-Narayana and Mohini throws lights on the deep-rooted psychology of sexual and gender pluralism in Indian consciousness. These concepts show that male identity is often transferred to female identity and vice-versa. As well, these mythologies or tales represents Indian mentality accepting sex-change and sexual pluralism. What one needs to do is to recognise that sex-changes or gender pluralism was part of the routine socio-cultural life of Indian society.

In Mahabharata, there is a very interesting characterisation of the concept of sex-change. According to the story, Shikhandini or Shikhandi was born as a girl to Drupada but was raised as a boy. On the wedding night, the wife of Shikhandi realised that her husband is a woman and she insulted her female husband. Unable to withstand the abuse, Shikhandi fled the palace and appealed anYaksha (divine being) to save her. The Yaksha accepted Shikhandi's feminity and donated his masculinity to her. Shikhandi is the classic example for sex-change and gender pluralism in ancient Indian civilisation. One is born as a girl but raised as a boy and then exchanges sex at a particular juncture. Similarly, Arjun, the archer hero of Mahabharata is another example for sex-change. According to the story, Arjun was cursed by the nymph named Urvashi that Arjun would be a third-gender. Subsequently, Arjun becomes Brihannala and lived in the Kingdom of Virata for an year.

Of all the mythologies associated with sex-change, the story of Ila is the most prominent one. According to the myth, Ila becomes a man and woman each month. Ila happens to marry god Budha (Mars), the planet god and they enjoy family life when Ila turns to be a woman. This classic example should remind us of psychological theories arguing that masculinity and feminity can be possessed by an individual at a time. Apart from these mythical stories, there are various gods and goddesses who are characterised as patrons of LGBTQs. The epic Ramayana gives a more vivid picture of transgender community. According to the story, while Rama was leaving for forest he requested his followers that 'all men and women' to return to the city. The hijaras did not feel bound by Rama's appeal and decided to follow him. Rama understood the position of hijaras and sanctioned them with the power to bless people at auspicious occasions.[11]

As demonstrated, a survey of ancient Indian texts can show sexual and gender pluralism along with sex-change in ancient times. Even though the historicity of these myths, legends and lore are doubtful, one may not be wrong to assume that plural forms of sexual behaviour, gender plurality and the dual nature of sexual identity in individuals were discussed in ancient India. Interestingly, there are texts indicating punishments for same-sex relations including homosexuality and lesbianism. Manusmrithi being one such work prescribing punishment for lesbian and homosexual relations.[12] Manusmrithi can be read as the indictor of brahmanic/ upper-caste regulations developed in later periods.This indicates that sexual and gender pluralism in ancient times had not been always accepted but were subject to ethical and moral problems. Apart from literature, there is a plethora of art works such as stone carvings, paintings and mural painting dealing with plural sexuality. Khajuraho group of monuments being a classic example for erotic sculptures. Majority of Khajuraho temples were built during the 10th and 11th century under the Chandela dynasty. The erotic artworks and stone carvings in these temple have been subject to multiple interpretations. What one needs to do with the erotic art forms of Khajuraho is to understand, on the one hand, that Indian society was open to sexual and gender pluralism. On the other, we need to be aware that lucid forms of sexual relations combined with complex social mechanisms provided social recognition for sexual and gender plurality in precolonial India. In the course of time, this trend received setbacks and restrictions on sexual and gender plurality were instituted.Two reasons are suggested for India's transition towards a monolithic sexual orientation instead of its earlier plural version. On the one hand, the establishment of Delhi Sultanate and Mughal dynasty redefined the forms of sexual orientation due to the Persian and Islamic ideologies the rise of colonialism drastically changed the pre-colonial sexual and gender plurality.

Colonialism and Gender/Sexual Plurality

The establishment of British colonialism and the subsequent influence of Western European values have problematised the concept of sexual pluralism in India. European concepts of sexual life have been influenced by a set of developments in Western Europe since the 16th century. Roman Catholic Church, Christian theology, especially its moral lessons, concepts of body, sanitation, asceticism and celibacy were some of the factors that shaped the Western orientation towards sexuality and body since 16th century. Through the discourses on body and sex western society created a monolithic pattern of human body and its sexuality. Michael Foucault, the post-structuralist scholar has showed the development of European notion of body and sex in the context of power and authority.[13] According to Foucault,

> "The appearance in nineteenth century psychiatry, jurisprudence and literature of a whole series of discourses on the species and subspecies of homosexuality, inversion, pederasty, and "psychic hermaphroditism" made possible a strong advance of social controls into this area of "perversity";[14]

As Foucault demonstrated, in the European schema of body and sexuality, various forms of sexual behaviours were labelled as either unnatural or abnormal. For the medieval European mind, homosexuality and lesbianism thus became criminal activities requiring punishments. The development of colonialism and science restructured the approaches towards sexual normalcy in social life.

With the rise of colonialism in India western values on sexual orientation and body were disseminated. The legal and authoritarian interventions by state and the missionary efforts problematised sexual and gender pluralism. Moral stories, advice and dress-codes prescribed by missionaries to the common folk to maintain bodily purity and sexual decency can be seen as efforts to institute a new outlook towards sex and body. The outbreak of Shannar rebellion in Travancore during the 1840s can be seen as an example for the influence of colonial values on human body and their sexuality. In India, the brahmanic form of social regulation had sanctioned lucid forms of sexual life for the non-brahmanic and especially the lower- castes. In the brahmanic schema of social life, lower-castes were not authorised to claim sexual purity since they have no bodily/ spiritual purity. Lucid form of sexual relations, especially being beneficial to the brahmanic patriarchy, was the norm in pre-colonial India. It was in this context that colonial interventions in the field of human body and sexuality, placing strict form of sexual conduct, gained momentum in India. First legal step towards this direction was materialised with the introduction of Indian Penal Code (IPC hereafter) in 1860. It remarks a notable era in the development of state-centered legal system in the country. While the IPC of 1860 formalised the procedure of Indian legal systems by codifying legal dictums, it also led to the establishment of an alien concept of body and sexuality in society. Indian Penal Code prescribed serious punishment for homosexuals or lesbians arguing that these sexual-behaviours were unnatural. Legal dictums on sexual behaviours were given in Section 377 of the Indian Penal Code in 1864. The law was based on the Buggery Act of 1533, and it was introduced to maintain regulated form of sexual relations in the country. Section 377 of the Indian Penal Code maintained that;

> "Whoever voluntarily has carnal intercourse against the order of nature with any man, woman or animal shall be punished with imprisonment for life, or with imprisonment of either description for a term which may extend to ten years, and shall also be liable to fine"[15]

For almost a century, Section 377 of IPC has been followed without any major challenges in India. Similar to Section 377 of IPC, the Criminal Tribe Act of 1871 was a harmful development with regard to the freedom and life of transgenders in colonial India. The Act of 1871 defined transgenders as criminals and instructed local governments to keep the transgenders under surveillance.[16] According to the Act, transgenders could be arrested without warrant and sentenced to imprisonment up to two years or fine or both.[17] The Act of 1871 clearly expresses the colonial approaches towards transgenders which sought to criminalise 'abnormal' forms of sexual orientation and gender plurality for governmental purpose. Already in 1865, R. Simson, the Secretary to the NWP Government had written to the Inspector General of Police that they wanted "to prevent an increase in the number of eunuchs and thus gradually lead to their extinction".[18]

For almost two centuries, Section 377 and the Act of 1871 were used to regulate the sexual conduct of Indians. Along with legal maxims, the imagination of 'normal sex' necessitated the marginalisation of LGBTQs in the country. However, the development of post-structuralist ideologies, feminism and the politics of post-war globalisation in the 1970s created favourable conditions for the development of LGBTQ movements. At the international level, movements for the rights of LGBTQs have gained momentum since 1960s. The South African Constitution prohibited discrimination on the basis of sexual orientation. Similarly, Scandinavia has equal rights for sexual minorities and any discrimination is seen as unconstitutional. Monica Tabengwa and Nancy Nicol have demonstrated how the development of sexual rights and LGBTQ movement can contribute towards gender justice in the context of Botswana.[19] By 1980s the issue of LGBTQ has become a visible identity problem in India.[20] Allen Ginsberg has pointed that the city of Calcutta had a thriving social network of gay people since 1960s.[21] 'Bombay Dost', the first gay magazine was published in 1980 from Bombay which raised LGBTQ issues to the forefront. Earlier, in 1977 Shakuntala Devi had published a study on homosexuality and it put forth the neglected sphere of LGBTQ world in India.[22] Following the publication of Bombay Dost, a collective named Sakhi was started in Delhi for the rights of LGBTQs. Apart from Bombay Dost and Sakhi, numerous collectives and magazines dealing with LGBTQ issues were published throughout the 1980s and 1990s. Fun Club, Pravartak, Counsel Club were some of the important groups worked for the rights of LGBTQs.

With changes taking place at the international level and considering the mounting pressure from various LGBTQ movements, Section 377 of Indian Penal Code came under social and legal scrutiny in various times. In 2001, the Naz Foundation (India) Trust, a non-governmental organisation has filed a lawsuit in the Delhi High Court seeking legalisation of homosexuality. In this case a two-judge bench of Delhi High Court decided in 2009 that treating consensual homosexuality as a crime is a violation of fundamental rights. Similarly, in its landmark judgment in *National Legal Services Authority (NALSA) vs. Union of India* in 2013, legal recognition for hijras or transgenders was recognised by the Supreme Court of India which created the position of 'third gender'.[23] In *Suresh Kumar Koushal vs. Naz Foundation*, a two-judge bench of Supreme Court decided to reinstate Section 377 of I.P.C. However, in Navtej Sigh Joharvz Union of India in 2018, a 5 judge bench of Supreme Court decided to scrap Section 377, decriminalising homosexual intercourse between adults. The Supreme Court verdict is a milestone in the history of LGBTQ rights in India. However, Supreme Court verdict cannot overrule social prejudices or popular beliefs which needs social awareness and deep-rooted respect for democracy. Correspondingly, various activists have argued that the (Transgender Persons Protection of Rights) Bill (TPPR) would legitimise violence and discrimination against the LGBTQs.[24]

Conclusions

Homosexuality, lesbianism, bisexuality and transgender identity are not diseases requiring medical treatment. Various ancient societies had developed particular mechanisms to address the issues of plural forms of sexual identity and sexual intercourses. What is needed is a consensus to recognise social pluralism that there are various ways of social existence through different forms of sexual identities. Authority and normalisation were the bandwagons of colonialism. What colonialism tried to replace in India was to install a new sensibility and approaches towards the LGBTQs who were leading a comparatively unobstructed way of life. Since postcolonial India is guided by colonial legacies, new forms of marriage, sex, family, institutions and medical knowledge on body and sexuality continued to govern Indian social consciousness. While hijaras or eunuchs are given a different position in mainstream Indian society, it is true that sexual and psychological abuse of these sections continues in India. It is fortunate that new openness with regard to sexual intercourse is developing in India recognising that the colonial restrictions on sexuality is only an extension of eighteenth century European legal system. Colonial mentality cannot be overthrown overnight but certainly they can be challenged and replaced. The recent verdicts on Section 377 and LGBTQ related cases points towards this direction.

References

1. Gloria Wekker. *White Innocence: Paradoxes of Colonialism and Race*, Duke University Press, 2016.
2. Johan Galtung. "Violence, Peace and Peace Research", *Journal of Peace Research*, Vol. 6, No. 3, 1969, pp. 167-191.
3. For more see, Elizebeth Kolsky. *Colonial Justice in British India: White Violence and the Rule of Law*, Cambridge University Press, 2011.
4. Frantz Fanon. The Wretched of the Earth, NBY: Grove Press, 1963, pp. 210-11.
5. For more see, Jose Ignacio Cabezon. Sexuality in Classical South Asian Buddhism, Somerville: Wisdom Publications, 2017, pp. 20-21.
6. Werner Menski, Comparative Law in a Global Context: The Legal Systems of Asia and Africa, Cambridge: Cambridge University Press, 2005, pp. 239-40.
7. *Ibid.*
8. Banarjee, AC. 1984. English Law in India, New Delhi; Abhinav, p. 288. Reproduced in Werner Menski, Comparative Law in a Global Context: The Legal Systems of Asia and Africa, Cambridge: Cambridge University Press, 2005, p. 263.
9. Jessica Hinchy. The Long History of Criminalizing Hijras, Himal-South Asian, 2nd July, 2019.
10. Anuradha Parasar. Homosexuality in India- The Invisible Conflict, Research paper available at www.delhihighcourt.nic.in
11. National Legal Services Authority (NALSA) vs. Union of India. Available at www.indiakanoon.org
12. Kalpana V Jawale. Issues and challenges of 'LGBT' minority people in India, International Journal of Applied Research, 2016; 2(6): pp. 408-410.
13. Michel Foucault. History of Sexuality Volume I: An Introduction, London: Allen Lane, 1979.
14. *Ibid.*
15. Section 377 of Indian Penal Code, 1860.
16. Jessica Hinchy. The Long History of Criminalizing Hijras, Himal-South Asian, 2nd July, 2019.
17. National Legal Services Authority (NALSA) vs. Union of India.

18. Jessica Hinchy, *op.cited.*
19. Monica Tabengwa with Nancy Nicol. The development of sexual rights and the LGBTQ movement in Botswana, pp. 339-358.
20. Bina Fernandez (Eds). Humjinsi: A Resources Book on Lesbian, Gay and Bisexual Rights in India, India Centre for Human Rights and Law, Mumbai, 1999, p. 101
21. *Ibid,* p. 102.
22. Kalpana V Jawale. Issues and challenges of 'LGBTQ' minority people in India, International Journal of Applied Research, 2016; 2(6): 408-410.
23. Times of India 15 April, 2014.
24. Jessica Hinchy, *op.cited.*

8

The Transgender Paradigm Shift Towards Freedom

— *Dr. Nisha Jolly Nelson*

"I am not pretending to be someone else,
***I'm tired** of pretending to be **someone I'm not...**"* **(Maya)**

Introduction

In a recent special issue of 'International Sociology', 'Gender matters: Studying Globalisation and social change in the 21st century', Chow (2000) argues that, mainstream theorising about globalisation (ignores) how globalisation shapes gender relationships and people's lives materially, politically, socially, and culturally at all levels. In the new global world the state is able to provide space to understand discuss and intervene at the manifestations of gender identity of transgender community in India on grounds of their non-normative sexuality. (Davis, Evans and Lorber, 2010). Similarly, gender and identity are perceived differently in communities and its culture also varies in the changing world. Globally, development was gender blind until early 1970s. During the period, women's issues were included under people's development. It was during 1970s the process of development included women as part of development. The shift from Women in Development to Gender and Development began in late 1980s and early 1990s. It was after the Beijing Conference in 1995 that the Gender Mainstreaming became a new approach to development.

Background

Transgender is an umbrella term for persons who do not conform their gender identity, gender expression or behaviour to their assigned sex (sex determined by birth) but refers to their internal sense of being male, female or someone else. So they try to communicate their identity through behaviour, clothing, hairstyles or body language. Transgenders include trans-men & trans-women (whether or not they have undergone sex reassignment surgery or hormonal treatment or laser therapy, etc.), gender queers, and a number of socio-cultural identities, such as kinnars, hijras, aravanis, jogtas, etc. (Aneesh, 2017).

Gender identity is one's internal sense of whether an individual is a male or a female. But when an individual is a transgender, this innate feeling contradicts with the actual sex. Then, the individual's body is either male or female but inside they are really the opposite sex. Thus, the individual feels 'trapped' in the wrong body. The so called 'trapped' feeling may begin either in infancy stage or when there are adults. When they discover the identity crisis during infancy, they may not disclose to others despite the fear and chaos as they are unaware of what is happening to them. Even if they disclose their identity to their family, some of them are not accepted in the family, schools and in the society. Due to the non-acceptance in the society, some of them wear the 'mask' and live as per others wish but in a dilemma of 'to be or not to be'; some of them breaks the chains and run away to chase their dream to reveal their identity. In such circumstances, a person feels that his or her body is not correct and the person will decide to have medical treatment, take hormones and undergoes surgery, to make the body suit according to his/her inner-self. People who undergo gender reassignment surgery to have these changes may be described as "transsexual."

Type of Transgenders

The Transgenders are known by different names in different places according to their culture.

They are commonly known as hijra, kothy, aravani and thirunangai, jogtas/jogappas, shivasakthy etc. (Aneesh : 2017).

(i) ***Kothi:*** They are a heterogeneous group who are described as biological males with feminine nature. Some Kothis are bisexual and get married to women. Most of them are poor and engage in sex work for their living. Some of the Hijras-identified people identify them as Kothis but all the Kothi-identified people do not identify themselves as transgender or Hijras (Ministry of Social Justice and Empowerment: 2014).

(ii) ***Aravanis and 'Thirunangi:*** In Tamil Nadu, Hijras are identified as "Aravani". Tamil Nadu Government has initiated a Welfare

Board for Aravanigal under the Department of Social Welfare. It defines Aravanis as 'biological males who self-identify themselves as a woman trapped in male's body'. Some of the Aravani activists desire that they may be called as 'Thirunangi' by the public and media. (Ministry of Social Justice and Empowerment : 2014)

(iii) Jogtas/Jogappas: Those persons who are dedicated themselves to serve as a servant of Goddess Renukha Devi (Yellamma) are Jogtas or Jogappas. Goddess Renukha Devi's (Yellamma) temples are in Maharashtra and Karnataka. 'Jogta' refers to a male servant of that Goddess and 'Jogti' refers to female servant (who is also sometimes referred to as 'Devadasi'). An individual can become a 'Jogta' or 'Jogti' their family agrees to their tradition or that individual finds a 'Guru' or 'Pujari' who accepts him/her as a 'Chela' or 'Shishya'. Mostly, the term 'Jogti Hijras' denotes those male-to-female transgender persons, devotees/servants of Goddess Renukha Devi and who are also in the Hijra communities. (Ministry of Social Justice and Empowerment : 2014)

(iv) Shiv-Shakthis: They are considered as males who are possessed by or particularly close to a goddess and who have feminine gender expression. Usually, Shiv-Shakthis are inducted into the Shiv-Shakti community by senior gurus, who teach them the norms, customs, and rituals to be observed by them. (Ministry of Social Justice and Empowerment: 2014)

(v) Hijras: They are biological males who reject their 'masculine' identity and identify either as women, or 'not-men' or 'in-between man and woman', or 'neither man nor woman'. If a Hijra has to be adopted by a Hijra Guru, then that person has to pay the membership fees to enroll oneself in a particular gharana (method school) to which that particular guru belongs to. It is mandatory that a hijra has to enroll in a gharana with which that individual adopts their customs and traditions. (Ministry of Social Justice and Empowerment: 2014)

Policy discourse

The Transgenders got recognition for the first time in India in the 2011 census. The 2011 Indian Census estimates the population of Transgenders to be over five lakhs and trans activists argues that the number is much higher. As per the census 2011 in India, Uttar Pradesh has the highest Transgender population in the country, which is One lakh thirty seven thousand four hundred and sixty four i.e., 1,37,464. In India, transgender people are visible in public, ridiculed in crude comedy in popular cinemas, shunned and feared but tolerated at rituals where their presence is supposed to be auspicious. The Transgender community faces social discrimination and social stigma in the society which leads to depression and suicides when they are isolated in the society. Hence, an awareness programme should be done to create public awareness to accept Transgenders as they are and not to harm and isolate them. Mainstreaming them to the forefront requires immense efforts from the government as well as the public and to protect their 'human rights'.

In India, the first initiative towards the remedial measures came in by the Judgment dated 15th April, 2014 by the Honorable Supreme Court in what is known as the NALSA verdict recognised 'transgender' as a gender identity and called for immediate remedial action. The act of Honorable Supreme Court brought in hope in the transgender community and among their supporters but the pace of change is gradual.

The Transgenders Persons (Protection of Rights) Bill, 2016

> *"Seldom, our society realises or cares to realise the trauma, agony and pain which the members of Transgender community undergo, nor appreciates the innate feelings of the members of the Transgender community, especially of those whose mind and body disown their biological sex. Our society often ridicules and abuses the Transgender community and in public places like railway stations, bus stands, schools, workplaces, malls, theatres, hospitals, they are sidelined and treated as untouchables, forgetting the fact that the moral failure lies in the society's unwillingness to contain or embrace different gender identities and expressions, a mindset which we have to change."-* ***(Judgement of the Honorable Supreme Court of India on 15 April 2014)***

The Transgender Rights Bill 2016 is based on a PIL filed by National Legal Services Authority (NALSA) urging the court to give separate identity to transgenders by recognising them as third category of gender. The Transgender bill was passed unanimously in the Rajya Sabha, or the upper house of the Indian Parliament, in April 2015. At that point, the government said that it would be brought into the lower house after it had "correct[ed] infirmities" and circulated its own revised draft among ministries. This process began in March 2016, when the draft Transgender Rights Bill 2016 was circulated by the Ministry of Social Justice and Empowerment for inter-ministerial consultation for two weeks. Although the comments were inadequately forthcoming, the bill was sent to the law ministry (prior to being sent for cabinet approval) in April. It said that Section 377 of IPC is being misused by police and other authorities against them and their social and economic condition is far from satisfactory. (Ministry of Social Justice and Empowerment: 2014).

- The Bill defines a transgender person as one who is partly female or male; or a combination of female and male; or neither female nor male. In addition, the person's gender must not match the gender assigned at birth, and includes trans-men, trans-women, persons with intersex variations and gender-queers.
- A transgender person must obtain a certificate of identity as proof of recognition of identity as a transgender person and to invoke rights under the Bill.
- Such a certificate would be granted by the District Magistrate on the recommendation of a Screening Committee. The Committee would comprise a medical officer, a psychologist or psychiatrist, a district welfare officer, a government official, and a transgender person.
- The Bill prohibits discrimination against a transgender person in areas such as education, employment, and healthcare. It directs the central and state governments to provide welfare schemes in these areas.
- Offences like compelling a transgender person to beg, denial of access to a public place, physical and sexual abuse, etc. would attract up to two years' imprisonment and a fine.

Transgender Policy in Kerala, 2015

The Judgment by the Honorable Supreme Court has also directed the Centre and State Government to grant legal recognition of their identity. As a result of the recognition of 'Third Gender' by the Honorable Indian Supreme Court verdict 2014, affirming the transgender community's freedom from discrimination and right to equality Kerala is the first State to establish a Policy for Transgenders, in India. As per the Census conducted in Kerala during 2015-16 there are One thousand and one hundred eighty seven Transgenders in Kerala. More of them are reluctant to reveal their identity. (Seetharaman, 2015). Transgenders are very much struggling for their day to day life activities. This group needs more attention for mainstreaming into the society. The survey report reflected the pitiable status of

Transgenders in Kerala. The survey of over four thousand Transgenders in Kerala estimated the Transgender population in Kerala to be twenty five thousand which is over 6 times higher than the Census 2011 estimate. According to the survey by the Department of Social Justice, Government of Kerala:

- 58 percent of Transgender students dropout before completing 10th grade.
- 54 percent had a monthly income of less than 5000 Rupees.
- 11.6 percent have regular jobs.
- 28 percent have been sexually harassed or raped by partners within 1 year.
- 96 percent do not file complaints against violence because of their gender identity.
- 51 percent of respondents were denied equal treatment in clinics and hospitals.
- 52 percent face harassment from the police.
- 81 percent wish to change their identity but have no support to change their physical appearance.
- 78 percent have kept their gender identity a secret at work for fear of discrimination. (State Policy of Transgenders in Kerala: 2015)

Hence, the survey in Kerala unveils the reality that more than half of transgender kids are dropped out of school before 10th grade and three-fourths keeping their gender identity a secret at work for fear of losing their job. It is understood that many Transgenders do not reveal their affirmed gender for fear of ostracisation and retribution.

The policy includes the right to equality, right to freedom of expression, right to dignity and a life without violence, and the right to equal voice and participation in development.

The Problem

The sex of an individual by birth which is the assigned identity may sometimes differ with the real identity in some persons. They struggle to live as per the assigned identity but in some circumstances, they reveal their actual identities which might be mistaken by others. If the individual performs as per the expectation of a community, then the self-identity and the identity assigned by the community would be related. But if the individual deviates from the identity assigned by the community, then there occurs a conflict of identity with the individual. The identity crisis may also lead to a different culture in the communities which may be accepted by them or rejected and isolate those individuals. They may have a guilt feeling of "not fitting in" with people of their assigned sex or are unable to perform the gender roles expected by the society. So they either run away from their native place and they become school dropouts, to find a shelter in other states and live with their real identities. The lack of education in some Transgender, forces them to fall into prostitution or beggary to earn their living. On the other way, others become aware of their transgender identities even from their childhood and show the courage to come out of their 'trapped body' or false identity. Those transgender who are ready to face their struggles and challenges bravely have proved to be successful in life and they 'live of their choice as they dreamed of'. Even while Kerala has shown great commitment in ideating and implementing gender mainstreaming through its policies, the question remains that whether the state has succeeded in translating Transgender policy into development practice. The first part of the article tries to understand Transgender Policy and the current status of its implementation drawing from secondary sources. It also tries to understand the state policy with respect to transgender community and to understand the contribution of state policies in bringing out change in discourses of gender identity in the State. The second par with empirical evidences draws into the plight of transgenders in Kerala.

Approach and Method

My interest to know transgender community and about their lives are due the opportunity I gained as part of the announcement made by our college as a transgender inclusive campus during the transgender remembrance day, 2015. Our college (Loyola College of Social Sciences, Thiruvananthapuram, Kerala) is the first in the State to proclaim publicly that it is a transgender inclusive campus. During this time I had the opportunity to meet transgenders and converse with them for long time as the Department of Sociology (the department in which I am associated with) initiated this event. Lot of transgender participants were present during the function. Drawing from the case studies and focus group discussion with the transgender community the article intends to open up a line of enquiry into the multifaceted dimensions of transgender including self perception of the individuals, sexual orientation and relationships, and the discrimination face by transgenders with a view to understand and document the unheard lives of the community. More specifically, it seeks to throw insights into the many problems faced by them due to their gender status and to arrive at suggestions to live a dignified life in the society. I followed Hollway and Jefferson's (2000) 'narrative approach' in which 'the researcher's responsibility is to be a good listener and the interviewee is a story-teller rather than a respondent'. A narrative approach enables a move away from a rigid 'question and answer' style of interview and allows the interviewer to flexibly respond to the narrator. One of the central characteristics of the narrative interview is that questions are open-ended so that 'stories' may be told. The researcher does not intervene until the respondent stops talking and then asks further questions to follow up on the developing themes. Even if the case is not representative of all transgender it does briefly show the kinds of experiences that is faced by transgender. Focus group discussion helped to identify different issues and problems faced by the community and some suggestions from among them to lead a quality life. A comprehensive literature review was done to understand the present gender identity status and policy for transgender people in India. The names used are pseudonyms to protect the identity of the individuals.

Case 1: Tessa was born at Kollam and studied upto pre-degree but could not complete her studies and wish to continue the same with the help of Kerala Saksharatha Mission's Continuing Education Programme. She has a mother, a brother and sister in her family. Tessa identified her identity from 5 years of age, she wanted to wear frocks for Onam celebration at home. They were very supportive from childhood onwards and she did not feel any discrimination in her family and even in school. During childhood, she wanted to play with girls rather than cricket with boys. Some of the ill comments while walking in the public hurted her but she ignored them patiently as she has no time to quarrel with them and she utilised her time productively to achieve her dream in life an artist. She got her lucky break through by assisting Ambikapillai at Wills India Fashion Week, which was one of her turning points in the make-up career. She is 42 years old now and she resides in Cochin. She is Kerala's first 'celebrity and bridal' transgender makeup artist, with an exceptional and unique style has reached audiences in a range of mediums, from magazine covers to feature films, ad films and films. She began her career before 22 years in make-up industry as female make-up and bridal make-up artist. Now doing make-up works in India and abroad, for numerous celebrities, models and brides. According to Tessa, *"Though Kerala has become more trans-friendly on paper, we are still discriminated against. So the attitude towards transgender has to change but it takes time."*

Case 2 : Gender swap marriage of Maria and John

John was born as a girl named Biji and now changed the identity as a man, who is now 46-year-old. Hails from Kottayam, Kerala, he now lives in Bangalore with his life partner Maria a transwoman from Kerala. John said that he was trapped inside a woman's body for years and undergone a gender reassignment surgery at a Mumbai hospital and there he met Maria, 22, a man who underwent surgery at the same clinic to become a woman. Both of them said that it was difficult to live with the false identity during their childhood. John told that he had long hair just like girls at the age of 13 but he felt from inner self that he was different. He liked to sit with girls while in the classroom but the girls felt scared by his attraction to them. He informed his mother that he wanted to be a 'boy' and his mother took him to a Doctor who said that such problems were just part of the onset of puberty due to the hormonal imbalances. Doctor recommended John to wait for some years before undergoing treatment. John had gender identity disorder (GID) a condition in which there is conflict between the gender assigned at birth and the gender the person identifies with, and it became severe day by day. Unfortunately, his mother passed away and his father re-married and he had to take the responsibility to look after his siblings rather than solving his own problems. John could fulfill his desire only at the age of 45 and now he is a male.

Maria 22 years old beautiful Transwomen who belongs to Kerala now resides in Bangalore confronted that she also experienced GID during childhood. After her father passed away, her mother took her to a doctor who advised to start hormone therapy to remain as 'boy'. As a result of the therapy, his facial and body structure changed and developed muscles, his shoulders became broader and she lost her hair too. She said "No one understood what I was going through. During my Class 10 board exams, I fainted owing to the pressure," She dropped out of school, studied software engineering and now works as a freelance web developer. Now, John and Maria got legally married this year but the traditional wedding is yet to come as they are waiting for Marias surgery to be completed. He adds that he and Maria wishes to do counselling for children who are experiencing GID. He said gender reassignment surgery costs between Rs18 lakh to Rs19 lakh in places such as Thailand, where it is popular. In India, it costs between Rs 4 lakh to Rs 5 lakh. Maria is a self-learner and she learned web designing on her own and now she works as a freelance Web developer in Bangalore. According to John and Maria, the transgenders are also human beings and they must be given equal opportunities and rights as other individuals.

Case 3: A Transgender poetess in Kerala

The person is a Transgender activist and of the opinion that most of the transgender people of the State are migrating to other States in the country because of the social ostracism here. Explaining the identity crisis and human rights violations being faced by the transgender community in the State, the activist said that awareness on the issues being faced by the minority groups is inevitable. She feels that she gets more acceptances in the society when she became a women.

VERBATIM NARRATIVES

(Issues emerged from Focus Group discussion)

The life of Hijras is much stressed now. When I say these things nobody will believe. Police come and torture us. Goons beat us and forcefully push into cars and make them do unsafe sex-to say openly without condom. They don't know the side effects that follow.

We live in constant fear. Beating, torturing and causing blood injuries are common things. When we say "these people don't believe us" I have heard lot of painful comments from the women than men. Women can't accept us or they never try to understand our feelings. They are very critical of our gender status and always look us in contempt

Our life is not secure. When we go out we are not sure whether we will come back. Our life is full of miseries.

I want to live a respectful life. I don't want to live in the margins. I want to live with the people among one. I want to live in the mainstream society.

I had to run away from here (Kerala) only because of the society and my parents. I fled when I was 16 as I was unable to stand the insult and contempt. I want to live as a woman. I don't want the next generation to suffer like me. So I will fight as long as I am able for the rights of my people.

We should also be treated like human beings. Why can't you see us like human beings? We are also born from a mother's womb. We need support from the society and government. Please help us !

Accept us in Kerala the way Tamil Nadu, Karnataka and Maharashtra government accepted us. Let us also live in Kerala. Please don't force us to run away from our place.

In Kerala, people had a general misconception about us. They think we are all sex workers. They are all scared of us and treat us with aversion. At work place we have to do overtime work, get less salary, sent out with various works in order to avoid the presence in the office and was often asked to change the way of dressing into formal ways (while respondent preferred feminine styles of dressing like jeans & kurta), as the employer expected.

Many of us are forced to marry. But I can't never love a woman as wife and perform the role of a husband and give love and care which a woman may expect. Forcing to marry had lead to many suicide cases in our community.

We face lot of issues from the public. People stare at us and tell we are sex workers. We cannot participate in any social functions like marriage, housewarming, engagement, and other ceremonies because of the fear of avoidance and humiliation. They use to call bad words and call some names.

I tried to commit suicide when I lost my job and my love due to my gender identity. I was severely depressed and mentally down.

We are not free to dress as we wish. So we often dress secretly as a woman/man when there are only transgender people around us. We are undergoing social exclusion, identity crisis and many other challenges in society. We have to hide our transgender identity to protect ourselves. We are called by various names like nine, chakka, elevens and chanthupottu. We are sexually and physically abused by people.

We always need social security and support from society because every day we encounter a number of problems. Sometimes we are beaten up by the public and police. We are ill treated at hospitals and at offices. Many of us do not have any source of income.

The above statements are some of the concerns and issues expressed in the focus group discussion by the transgender in the study. This shows the range of difficulties and discrimination face by them and it's visible from the statements that their basic human rights are being violated. Their shattered dreams and hopes, the tear filled eyes all portrays the amount of pain they have to experience in their everyday life. Discrimination and harassment are persistent. Even though public awareness and acceptance of transgender individuals has been gradually improving, there is still a long way to go in ensuring adequate services are available to this community to fight against discrimination, harassment and social stigmatisation they face.

Discussion

Intervention of Transgender Policy in Kerala

As Kerala became the first state to announce a transgender policy in 2015, Kerala marked the name in history books for framing a transgender policy and implementing it. The policy covered trans-men, trans women and intersex individuals. It ensures that the transgender community is given equal opportunities to live and sustain in the society. With the introduction of Transgender Policy in Kerala, there are many changes in the transgender community which are enlisted below:

- *The Transgenders voted for the first time in Kerala Election*: Two persons of the 'third gender' voted in the assembly elections in Kerala last year. Surya, an artist and Suji are the only two who are listed as 'third gender' in the state electoral roll casted their first vote as 'transgenders'. We can consider this vote as a proof for the society's recognition of the transgender society.
- *First school for Transgenders opened in Kerala:* The Sahaj International School in Kerala with the support of National Open School (NOS) was inaugurated in December 30, 2016 in Kochi to give education for Transgenders.
- *Transgenders Sports Meet :* Kerala State Sports Council organised the first state-level sports meet for Transgenders. The participants included more than 100 TGs from 14 districts in Kerala. It is the first time that a state has conducted a state-level sports meet for TGs. If more states conduct such sports meet, then TGs could participate in National and International sports meet in future.
- *Employment in Kochi Metro Railway:* Kochi Metro Rail Ltd. had decided to extend job opportunities for transgenders in housekeeping, customer relations and crowd management. They have recruited 23 TGs in Kochi Metro Railway.
- *Transgender employed in MNC :* Zara Sheikha, a Trans woman is the first TG to get a job in an MNC in UST Global broke convention in Thiruvananthapuram. The move by the MNC shows the attitude of breaking stereotypes. (Jacob : 2017)
- *State Transgender Justice Board in Thiruvananthapuram*: The board has held its first meeting on July 5, 2017. Social Justice Minister K.K. Shylaja is the Chairperson of the board. 6 members are from TG community and other members include Secretaries of Home, Finance, Education, Law, Culture, Health, and Local

Self-Government departments; directors of Social Justice and Public Instruction and a representative of a non-governmental organisation for transgenders. According to sources in the Social Justice Department, the board will monitor the implementation of the policy and coordinate with various departments to ensure that the schemes are executed effectively to reach its beneficiaries. The meeting of the Board also discussed about issuing ID cards to all the registered TGs in Kerala, to offer legal awareness to transgenders to avoid the crimes against them, 24/7 helpline for TGs is also in the pipeline and a certificate will be given to the TGs specifying their gender for legal documents. (The Hindu : 2017)

- *Mainstreaming in Politics:* Recently, CPI(M)'s youth wing Democratic Youth Federation of India (DYFI) initiated the membership for transgenders in Thiruvananthapuram and it is the first time in history that Transgenders are given membership in a political party. Out of the 11 members in the DYFI unit, 9 of them are transgenders. The party declared that the act of membership given to the TGs is done as a part of its efforts to bring the marginalised section into mainstream politics.
- *Consideration in PSC exams:* On October 25, 2017, Kerala High Court announced that Transgenders shall write PSC examinations as females. Yet another milestone in the history of transgenders in Kerala.
- *Mainstreaming of Transgenders in Arts and Media :*
    - o Dhwayah Arts and Cultural Society organised the first transgender beauty pageant in Kerala. Like other beauty contests, participants had gone through auditions and grooming sessions. Almost 40 trans-women took part in the contest and 15 of them reached the final round. The opportunity gave the TGs a confidence and self-esteem and a sense of socially acceptance.
    - o A Trans woman, Deepthi was featured in Vanitha for the first time in 2016. The story in Vanitha magazine gave an awareness to the public on the transgenders and the struggle she had to face for her transformation from a man to a woman.
    - o A Trans woman, Anjali Ameer was casted in a lead role in a Malayalam movie with actor Mammootty. It is the first time that a Trans woman will be acting in a lead role in Malayalam film industry.

- o Sharmila Nair, a fashion designer from Kochi selected 2 TGs to be models to portray her new saree collection 'Mazhavil' which she dedicated to TG community. The 2 Trans women models were Maya Menon and Gowri Savithri.

From the above, it is understood that with the intervention of the policy for Transgenders, Kerala has witnessed many transgender friendly initiatives recently to bring the minority group into mainstream of the society. The government had earmarked Rs 10 crore for their welfare in the last budget. The State Poverty Eradication Mission, Kudumbashree, had also formed an Exclusive neighbourhood group for the empowerment of transgenders. The government would arrange special classes with assistance from the civic authorities and continuing education centres for transgenders in each district.

Conclusion

The study understood the significance of Kerala's Transgender Policy in the present scenario. With the launch of transgender policy in Kerala, the Transgenders find a horizon of hope and happiness when they are given their space in society by government and they have a positive feeling of 'acceptance'. Earlier, the Malayali hijras were found in Tamil Nadu, Maharashtra and Andhra Pradesh, but not in Kerala. With the intervention of policy, the TGs wish to live in Kerala due to the social acceptance and job opportunities offered to them in Kochi Metro, PSC and membership in political parties. This is a positive sign of transition of culture and identities. People are given the freedom to remain and live as they are and they wish to be. While Tamil Nadu, Maharashtra and West Bengal have Transgender Welfare Boards, Kerala's Policy goes beyond welfare and encourages a rights-based approach.

From the experience of the transgender community it can be concluded that even if we have a policy still transgenders are faced with numerous problems which needs to be addressed by several stakeholders. It needs variety of solutions and actions. The societal mindset need to be changed so that the negative attitude and prejudice towards the transgenders can be changed. But this will take long time as social change happens at a slow pace. Attitude of government, general public and health-care systems and practice require change.There needs to be greater awareness regarding gender diversity in families, in public spaces, educational institutions, in healthcare and among law enforcement authorities including police.

References

Aneesh, M.S. 2017. *Social Exclusion of Physically Disabled Transgenders (M To F) In Kerala. Int. J. of Adv. Res. 5(4). 1-6] (ISSN 2320-5407).* Retrieved from www.journalijar.com

Davis, K., Evans, M. and Lorber, J. 2010. *Handbook of gender and women's studies*. London : Sage.

Esther Ngan-ling Chow. 2003. Gender Matters: Studying Globalisation and Social Change in the 21st Century. *International Sociology*. Volume: 18 issue: 3, page(s): 443-460.

Government of India, Census 2011.co.in>transgender.

Hollway, W. and Jefferson, T. 2000. Doing Qualitative Research Differently. Free Association, Narrative and the Interview Method, London: Sage.

Jacob, Shalin. June 24, 2017. *9 Times Kerala. Pioneered With Its Transgender Policies & Showed The World How It's Done.* Scoop Whoop. Retrieved from https://www.scoopwhoop.com

Ministry of Social Justice and Empowerment. 2014. Report of the Expert Committee on the Issues relating to Transgender Persons. New Delhi. Government of India. Retrieved from http://socialjustice.nic.in

Nanda, Serena. 1999. *Neither Man nor Woman: The Hijras of India.* Ontario, Canada: Wardsworth Publishing Company

National AIDS Control Organisation. National Behaviour Surveillance Survey: Men who have sex with men injecting drug users. New Delhi: Ministry of Family and Health Welfare. Government of India, 2006.

PTI. October 1, 2017. *CPI(M)'s youth wing opens doors for transgenders.* The Indian Express. Retrieved from http://indianexpress.com

Rajesh, and Naved, A. 2013. Approach paper on education and employment opportunities and challenges for transgender. Ministry of Social justice and Empowerment. New Delhi: Government of India.

Reddy, G., & Nanda S. 2009. Hijras: An alternative Sex/Gender in India. In C.B. Brettel C.F. Sargent, Gender in cross cultural perspective. Upper Saddle River, New Jersey: Pearson-Prentice Hall.

S. Nanda. 1996. "Hijra." Encyclopaedia of World Cultures. [Online]. Available: http://www.encyclopedia.com/doc/1G2-3458000491.html

Seetharaman, G. 2015. *What Kerala's new transgender policy could teach other states about recognising the rights of a maltreated community*. The Economic Times. Retrieved from https://economictimes.indiatimes.com

Sen, I. 2005. *Human Rights of Minority and Women's*, (Transgender Human Rights), Delhi: Isha Books, Vol. 2, pp. 4-41.

Staff Reporter. June 29, 2017. *Need for awareness among officials stressed.* The Hindu. Retrieved from www.thehindu.com

State Policy of Transgenders in Kerala. 2015. Social Justice Department. Retrieved from www.kerala.gov.in

Sujata, Sen. 2012. (ed) *Gender Studies*. Dorling Kindersley (India) Pvt. Ltd. Licensees of Pearson Education in South Asia.

www.thehindu.com>article4413780

www.undp.org>HIV_and_development Hijras/Transgender women in India: HIV, Human Rights and Social Inclusion UNDP. India, 2010.

9

Disinclination and Discrimination Towards Third Sex in the Society

—Athira G.J

Abstract

There are two ways to reveal your identity in terms of gender so far. Either a male or a female at your birth- society demands!! The genetic rules that resembles to me decides who I ama boy or a girl. What if, later on my life expedition I feel am not mentally or physically fit to live with the assigned identity. Here comes a new birth- Transgender. From the birth to death social structure decides who you are and what role you expected to perform based on gender. This paper looks in to the transgender issues in workplace and educational institutions and the need for empowerment. It is an attempt to address the general issues faced by the vulnerable sections of the society. This is an ideal topic that should be addressed, especially in this current runninng context of offering two seats in universities to transgender students and a stellar verdict usherded by Supreme Court Under Section 377 will be a facelift to them.

Keywords: *Education, Employment, Empowerment, Sec 377 IPC.*

Literature review

Brett Genny Beemyn (2004) depicted an international scenario of transgender community faced globally. If institutions are to be welcoming to people of all genders, issues of discrimination and equal access to facilities and healthcare need to be addressed.

Pramod Kumar (2014) reported an interactive session among the transgenders in the light of Supreme Court decision to accept transgender as the third gender. Real life complexities and the need for educational enhancement and skill development for better lifestyle were strongly pinpointed.

Michelle Dietert & Dianne Dentice (2009) carried out a research to provide accounts of the workplace experiences of male-identified transgender individuals or female-to-male (FTM) individuals. Study revealed that many micro level troubles for the participants stemmed from lack of support by management and intolerant behaviour by coworkers. The education of the general population about gender diversity is essential to promoting understanding and tolerance, along with legislation at the macro level to address discriminatory workplace practices.

West and Zimmerman (1987) suggest that gender is constructed by and for social interaction, with children learning very early what it means to be either a girl or a boy. This binary thinking about gender becomes entrenched in social institutions beginning with the family and extending to schools and the workplace. Binary gender arrangements are reinforced and reconfirmed when individuals engage in activities and behaviours such as those involving dress, the use of restrooms and locker facilities, and self-presentation to authority figures. Furthermore, societal gender identity expectations shape the gender roles one may assume.

Rise of Transgender

"Transgender" is an umbrella term describing individuals whose identity and/or gender expression does not reflect the societal gender norms associated with the sex assigned at birth. Until there is a federal law in place to protect transpeople in the workplace, discrimination directed at those who deviate from gender norms will likely continue. The issue is not a matter of allocating "special" rights to transgender people but rather one of allocating rights that are enjoyed by the society as a whole: the right to work in an environment free from harassment, fear, and discrimination.

This paper on the general perceptions and attitudes towards the transgender and the issues associated with them. More than a conceptual or descriptive paper, prior attention is to think and put forward certain issues known to us but we keep silence and act like rituals.

When gender matters?

Gender matters when appear on a college documents, including identification cards, transcripts, financial aid and employment forms, and enrollment records.

With an aim to bring the transgender community to the mainstreams the government decided to sanction two extra seats for transgender students.

The move is meant for all courses offered by the universities and recognised arts and science colleges in the state and will allow transgenders who have had to discontinue their studies for various reasons to now reapply and pursue their dreams.

Section 377 IPC

LGBT filed writ petition challenging the constitutional validity of Sec 377 of the Indian Penal Code as it violates their fundamental rights to life, autonomy and dignity guaranteed under Article 21, right to equality under Article 14 and right to expression and freedom under Article 19. Chapter XVI, Section 377 of the Indian Penal Code introduced during the British rule of India criminalised sexual activities "against the order of nature" including homosexual activities.

Sec 377 enumerates that- Whoever voluntarily has carnal intercourse against the order of nature with any man, women or animal, shall be punished with (imprisonment for life), or with imprisonment of either description for a term which may extended to ten years, and shall also be liable to fine (unnatural offences).

Issues to be addressed with respect to Sec 377.

The Transgender Persons (Protection of Rights) Bill, 2016

A Bill to provide for protection of rights of transgender persons and their welfare and for matters connected therewith and incidental thereto.

"Transgender person" means a person who is—

(a) neither wholly female nor wholly male; or

(b) a combination of female or male; or

(c) neither female nor male; and whose sense of gender does not match with the gender assigned to that person at the time of birth, and includes trans-men and trans-women, persons with intersex variations and gender-queers.

Act 2016 discuss different aspects like prohibition against discrimination, recognition of identity, welfare measures adopted by the government, obligation of other person and establishments, education, social security and health of transgenders, offence and penalties, and National Council for Transgenders.

Climate changed. Listen the people around us and listen their daily issues. There are different issues raised by the trans people in the society are given at a glance below:

- Conflict over a transitioning woman using the women's restroom. Another area where transgender people experience discrimination is in their use of public restrooms. The "bathroom issue" is particularly a problem for transsexual women.
- Transgender students who live in residence halls, especially single-sex dormitories, can face housing and roommate issues, as well as bathroom problems.
- Greater peer pressure to conform to gender norms, the almost complete lack of knowledge about transgender issues, and the oversight of generally conservative society and parents.
- Renting a house to a transgender is being a current running issue.
- Transgressive identities place transgender individuals in conflict with norm-driven societal institutions. The result is that these individuals are forced to deal with issues including but not limited to the following: access to surgery and healthcare coverage; policies that refuse changes to official documents such as birth certificates, social security cards, and drivers' licences; dress codes in public schools and the workplace; the rights to marry, to adopt children, and to take custody of children; immigration issues; and rejection by family and friends. Additionally, transgender people negotiate their own gender identity on a daily and, in some cases, moment-by-moment basis.

Conclusion

Staid rules still in the society that may cause and impose such huge restrictions to these people. Discrimination has been continuing in the name of race, class, colour, clan since the human evolution. But major issues raised by the trans group should be addressed seriously though they are becoming a minor session of the society.

References

Stryker, Susan, and Whittle, Stephen, eds. 2006. *The Transgender Studies Reader*. New York: Routledge.

Stryker, Susan. 2006. "(De)Subjugated Knowledges: An Introduction to Transgender Studies." In *Stryker, and Whittle, Transgender Studies Reader*.

Stryker, Susan. 2008. Transgender History. Berkeley, CA: Seal.

Valentine, David. 2007. *Imagining Transgender: An Ethnography of a Category*. Durham, NC: Duke University Press.

10

An Understanding of Transgenders' Life in Kerala

—Aswathy, A.K

Abstract

This paper gives a look into the life of transgenders in Kerala and the reality of Kerala Transgender Policy. Kerala, the state with highest Human Development Index was always been indifferent to the marginalised transgender community. Transgender people are the oppressed sect in the society. They are the potential target because of the widespread prejudices. Transgender individuals experience a number of direct and indirect discriminations. They face innumerable difficulties in their day-to-day existence such as barriers to accessing healthcare, social stigma and gender discrimination. A study is made here for the general understanding of transgenders' life in Kerala.

Introduction

'Gender identity' is defined as a personal conception of oneself which is intimately related to the concept of gender role (outward manifestations of personality that reflect gender identity). The difference lies in the fact that gender identity is self-identified whereas gender role is manifested within society. For example, if a person considers himself as a male and is most comfortable referring to his personal gender in masculine terms, then his gender identity is male. However, his gender identity is male only and only if he demonstrates typically male characteristics in behaviour and mannerisms.

In English language, the terms **'gender'** and **'sex'** are often used interchangeably which is wrong in medical sense. Biological Sex and Gender are different. **Sex** includes physical attributes such as external genitalia, sex chromosomes, gonads, sex hormones and internal reproductive structures. At birth it is used to assign sex, i.e. male or female. **Gender**, on the other hand is far more complicated. It is the complex interrelationship between an individual's sex, one's internal sense as well as one's outward presentation and behaviour.

Conventionally speaking, there are mainly two gender identities; masculine and feminine and it is often connected with the birth assigned sex (i.e. masculine for persons who are male by birth and feminine for the persons who are female by birth). Till recent time the term man was considered to denote only male. When we say a sentence, "man is a social animal", we perceive a meaning that a male is a social animal. When the feminist movements became powerful, society got the perception that the term "man", when used to denote human being includes women or females also. Like the women lived without any identity and individuality for centuries, there is a group of people who are "neither male nor female" living in our society. They live in social negligence and alienation in many countries. They are commonly termed as **LGBT (Lesbians, Gay, Bisexual, Transgender).** Transgenders are people who have a gender identity which is different from their birth assigned sex.

The term is sometimes used as an umbrella term to describe anyone whose identity falls outside of stereotypical gender norms. But more precisely, it refers to an individual whose gender identity does not match their assigned birth gender. In short, transgender is a term **"denoting or relating to a person whose sense of personal identity and gender does not correspond with their birth sex"** (Oxford Dictionary).

As said earlier, transgender is often used as an umbrella term that includes 'transsexual', 'gender queer', 'gender fluid' etc. But, mainly there are two divisions in transgender; **Male to Female (MtF)** and **Female to Male (FtM).** MtF are those persons who are male by birth but possesses a female gender identity while FtM are those who are female by birth but have a male gender identity. This clearly shows that transgender is a concept related to gender expressions rather than biological sex and being a transgender is independent of sexual orientation. They may identify themselves as heterosexual, bisexual etc. In short, it can be said that conventional sexual orientation labels are inadequate or inapplicable or inappropriate for them.

The term 'transgender' was first coined by **John F. Oliven** of **Columbia University** in his work, **'Sexual Hygiene and Pathology' (1965)**. While suggesting this new term, he said that the term which had previously been used, 'trans sexualism' was misleading as gender identity is beyond the concept of sexuality. The term transgender was then popularised by various transgender, transsexual and transvestite people. Now, people who wish to live without **Sex Reassignment Surgery (SRS)** are generally known as transgenders and those who undergo surgery are called transsexuals.

Most transsexual men and women suffer from great psychological and emotional pain due to the conflict between their gender identity and their original gender role and anatomy. The only recourse they find is to change their gender role and undergo gender reassignment therapy. This may include taking hormones or having Sex Reassignment Surgery (SRS) to modify their primary and secondary sexual characteristics. The requirements for hormone replacement therapy vary greatly. Often a minimum time period of psychological counselling is required, and a minimum time spent living in the desired gender role in order to ensure they can function psychologically in that role.

Medical science offers a scientific reason for the origin of gender that is a diffusion of both masculine and feminine. A foetus when formed is in a feminine state. Its sex can be determined as male or female only after six weeks. If the foetus receives the male hormone androgen, it develops the sexual organs of a male. In the second stage too, if it receives male hormone the feminine state of the foetus' brain is changed to masculine state. The unavailability of male hormone in second stage leads to the birth of a child who may be a male in physical appearance and female in gender expressions. The child may fall into the category of gay or transgender. The same is the case of a female child also. If the foetus receive male hormone in the second stage, it will lead to the birth of a child with female sexual organs and male gender identity. Being raised in the wrong gender causes them profound gender dysphoria and mental anguish as they grow up. Early theories were based on the belief that gender is a learned behaviour. People believed that transgenderism was a lifestyle choice and this belief led to the social stigma attached to the term. Some of the psychological factors which have been linked with transgenderism are parental rejection, absence of father during childhood, having emotionally-distant father, peer pressure, perfectionism, media images, self-rejection and poor self-esteem which may be reinforced by hostile reception from society.

Life of transgenders in Kerala: An overview

In the historical judgement on 15th April 2014, the Supreme Court of India observed that 'transgender community is treated by the society as "unnatural" and generally as objects of ridicule and even fear on account of superstition.' The judgement directed the Centre as well as State governments to ensure fundamental rights of the transgender communities all over the country. This was on account of the Constitutional guarantee of equality irrespective of gender. Transgenders were granted third gender status also. As followed by the above development, the then State Government of Kerala formulated a Transgender policy for the welfare of the transgender community of the state. The problems faced by the transgenders came to the mainstream Kerala by this development. The transgenders of Kerala prefer to hide their gender identity due to social stigma and fear of social negligence. This necessitates a deep study into the living conditions of this people and here lies the scope of our study.

The group of transgenders has been identified as the targets of discrimination in many spheres of their lives. This exposes them to tremendous social and economic insecurity. When the situation of transgenders in Kerala is taken into consideration, they are side-line from the mainstream. The concept of transgender got emphasised recently in Kerala thereby motivating transgender youth to reveal their gender identity. Years ago, they were forced to remain behind the walls of social stigma. They were not socially accepted because transgenders were considered as an "unusual creation". It can be implied that some people in this section have not yet revealed their identity as a third gender due to the fear of facing the world. Therefore, it is evident that transgenders are present among us in a large number, but they are invisible to the society.

The Transgender survey of 2014-15 highlighted that more than half of (58%) TGs dropout before completing 10th grade. There are several reasons for the dropouts before degree. Major among them are:

- Economic reasons; mainly poor financial conditions of families.
- Gender related negative experiences like physical and sexual abuse and mental harassment.
- Lack of interest and awareness about higher studies.

When we look into the marital status of transgenders, the majority stays single. The reasons they state for being single are family circumstances, financial background and their so called "abnormal behaviour". Some persons are not ready to marry without revealing their gender identity, which is impossible in present scenario. Some of them are married, some of them have kids. But the surprising fact is that these married people have not disclosed about their gender identity and the reasons pointed out include:

- Afraid about their acceptance by the society and family.
- Unaware about the fact that being TG is a normal case.

Many of them are staying alone. This is partially due to the lack of family support and partially by their will. Lack of support is due to the conventional "negative" attitude about the concept of third gender. The families lack awareness about the existence of transgenders. Also some families are restricted to give support due to fear of social seclusion. A surprising fact is that, many of the transgenders have not revealed their identity to their families. This is also because of the above reasons. Also some of the people of this section themselves have a negative attitude about the concept of transgenders. This is because of the notion among them that male and female is the only gender identities that can exist. In rural areas, it is considered that being a transgender is a sin of them. People assume that married life may change the so called "abnormal behaviour" of these people.

The recent trend reveals that nowadays, transgenders are not stepping back from the social sphere due to their gender identity. In general, transgenders face a positive approach while visiting the social spaces or while participating in the public events. One of the reason is the Transgender Policy that has been presented in the Legislative Assembly. Before the upcoming of policy, they were exposed to the abuses of officials as well as public. They have faced a negative approach from hospitals. This unveils the fact that they are not able to avail even the basic facilities in a humanitarian manner. They also had experiences of misbehaviour from the part of Police authorities. Even after the introduction of the Transgender Policy, there were reports of misbehaviour towards transgenders in Ernakulam where, two transgenders were arrested for no reason. In general, health and security being a basic necessity, is not properly ensured for them. On the contrary they face more abuse from these institutions. They are being humiliated by the public. This is mainly because of their so called "abnormal behaviour" according to the conventional rules of our society.

Many transgenders rely upon private sector jobs like security jobs, home nursing, petrol bunk staff and techno park staff. This trend implies;

- It is very difficult to acquire a job in the government sector these days, even as a male or female.
- Even, to get a job, they have to reveal their identity (as a transgender) or they should apply with a false identity (male or female) for

which they are not willing. Until 2015, government did not have a favourable approach towards them.

Other than private sector, some of them are self-employed as dancers, drama artists, makeup artists, fashion designers and related professions. In majority these occupations, transgenders were able to maintain their identity. Some of the samples have eloped from their families due to the harassments faced from the family members for being a transgender. This has denied them from having their own property.

The economic conditions of these people are somewhat in a better position in Kerala on contrary to the conditions prevailing all over in India. When the condition of India is taken into consideration, most of these people are sex workers and beggars. In Kerala, the transgender people are hesitant to reveal their identity. This helps them to sustain in their jobs, thus earning better incomes. These people face a worse condition in their social life.

Transgender people have been documented in many cultures and societies from antiquity until the present day. However, the meaning of gender variance may vary from culture to culture. Every society contains individuals who do not fit into the culture's dominant sex/gender categories. The transgender community, which is one such community, is subjected to series of human rights violations and is kept away from the mainstream of national life. The dominant discourse on human rights in the world has yet to come to terms with the production of absolute humane consideration of transgender communities.

The transgender community is subjected to violence and abuse mainly due to the absence of social concern. The central concern about the transgender community pertains to the societal violence inflicted on them. The media have also presented several reports and analyses about the attitude of family, society and state towards the transgender community. The parents have not understood the psychology of transgender community on the basis of humanitarian considerations and scientific values.

The parents and other family members are more concerned about the attitude of society which is based on the traditional value system. The aggrieved persons are made to leave the homes under painful and humiliating circumstances. The society also does not provide employment, shelter and security to the members of this community. They are forced to practice begging and enter the world of prostitution in order to survive in the society against several odds. The public and private institutions also refuse to give them shelter economically and otherwise due to the existing social stigma. The family members also let down the transgender persons in order to safeguard their social status. The police personnel also take them for granted and refuse to register cases in times of violation of human rights. Transgender children are subjected to abuse at home, at school or in their communities. A lifetime of this can be very challenging and can sometimes cause anxiety disorders, depression and other psychological illnesses.

The most common mental health issues transgender persons experience are depression as well as adjustment, anxiety, personality, and post-traumatic stress disorders. While the transgenders have even though gained more acceptance in our society, the stress of dealing with the confusion and society's negative response can lead to numerous other problems. They appear to be at risk for mental health problems like other persons who experience major life changes, relationship difficulties, chronic medical conditions, or significant discrimination on the basis of minority status. Many transgender patients experience distress and anxiety about their gender identity, and may have less familial and peer support as compared to non-transgender individuals.

Even after the implementation of a comprehensive transgender policy, they are deprived off their basic needs and rights. Issue of ration cards and identity cards to transgenders were introduced by the state government. But the implementation process is caught in the chains of red-tapeism.

Amidst of all these fallacies in transgender policy implementation, the issue has now been considered as one of the major problems of our society. Many positive changes are taking place with regard to the uplift of transgenders. For the first time in the history of Kerala, two transgenders voted in the assembly elections held on May 2016. They were issued transgender voter ID cards. Another main important change is establishing a school exclusively for transgenders. Kerala is first to have one such facility in India. One of Indias largest self-help groups for women, Kudimbashree, opened their first transgender section in Kerala. The Self-Help Group was formed with transgenders as its members in Kottayam district, one of the places with largest population of transgenders in the state.

Public should be made aware of the existence of transgender community and their issues. Only awareness can bring about a change in the conventional negative attitude. It was a great step to introduce a comprehensive policy to improve the living conditions of transgenders. But the implementation process was not that effective to make a revolutionary change in the society. For this, it could have been better if the policy was introduced as a bill that will enforce the people to abide it. The issuing process of ration cards and voter IDs for transgenders should be made more effective. Small and quick changes like introduction of a third gender column in all the official forms and records should be made possible. Education system must be restructured in a way that the next generation should accept such a community rather than marginalising these people. Transgender welfare boards should be implemented as early as possible. Most importantly, the transgender people should be made more aware about their rights and should be led to the mainstream so that they feel that they are also normal human beings.

Conclusion

Changes have been welcomed by the society for the improvement in the living conditions of transgenders. But these changes are not even as it occurs only in major cities in Kerala. The developments should be more comprehensive that it can motivate such sections of the society to come out of their unwanted shells. The welfare schemes for transgenders introduced by the Government of Kerala remain in paper only. If these proposed schemes have to ripe a fruitful result, they have to be implemented efficiently. Also, proper monitoring must be done in cases of implemented policies. Thus, only a strong push from the administrative level can initiate a positive change towards the uplift of marginalised transgender community in Kerala.

Rigveda says, **"unnatural is also natural"**. The saying says that whatever in this universe being called as unnatural is also natural. In the light of this sentence, transgenders are also to be treated as natural, not an "abnormal creation". Democracy is not the autocracy of majority. On the contrary, it is the rule of that majority who respects the rights of the minorities. The main distinction between the modern democracy and ancient democracy lies in this fact. So transgenders will get their rights when majority accepts it.

References

- Gagne, Patricia; Tewksbury, Richard and McGaughey, Deanna (1997). 'Coming Out and Crossing Over: identity Formation and Proclamation in a Transgender Community', *Gender and Society*, Vol. 11, No. 4, August 1997.
- Michelraj, M (2015). 'Historical Evolution of Transgender Community in India', *Asian Review of Social Sciences*, Vol. 4, No. 1, Jan-June 2015.
- Raju, Venkatrama D and Beena, K.S (2015). 'A Study on Socio-Economic Issues of Third Genders in Tamil Nadu', International Journal of Science and Research, Vol. 4, Issue 7, July 2015.
- Chakrapani, Venkatesan (2010), 'Hijras/Transgender Women in India: HIV, Human Rights and Social Exclusion', Issue Brief (December 2010), UNDP.

- Chettiar, Anitha (2015). 'Problems Faced by Hijras (Male to Female Transgenders) in Mumbai with Reference to Their Health and Harassment by the Police', *International Journal of Social Science and Humanity*, Vol. 5, No. 9, September 2015.
- Abbas, Tanveer; Nawaz, Yasir; Ali, Muhammad; Hussain, Nisar; Mushtaq, Shahzad Khaver; Nawaz, Rab (2014). 'Social Adjustment of Transgender: A Study of District Chinot, Punjab (Pakistan)', *Academic Journal of Interdisciplinary Studies*, Vol. 3, No. 1, March 2014.
- Human Rights Law network (2015). 'Issues Faced by Transgender Persons in Odisha: Fact-Finding Mission to Bhubaneswar and Cuttack'.
- National Centre for Transgender Equality and the National Gay and Lesbian Task Force (2009), 'National Transgender Discrimination Survey'.
- 'Transgender Survey Kerala 2014-15', Department of Social Justice, Kerala.
- '*Moonnam Lingam: Linganeethikkayulla Muravilikal*' (Editor:Shaji Joseph, Chintha Publications, Thiruvanathapuram)
- Suguna, M., (2015). Self-help groups a panacea for the socio-economic development of transgenders in Tamil Nadu.
- Golden Kisha, B., (2014). Psychosocial Problems of Transgenders and The Attitude of Society Towards Them.
- https://en.wikipedia.org/wiki/Gender_identity
- https://www.genderspectrum.org/quick-links/understanding-gender/
- https://emedicine.medscape.com/article/917990-overview#a1
- https://legbtqnation.com/2016/02/trans-history-101-transgender-expression-in-ancient-times
- https://www.theguardian.com/lifeandstyle/2010/jun/02/brief-history-transgender-issues
- https://en.wikipedia.org/wiki/Transgender_history

11

The Social Upliftment of Transgenders in Kerala through Employment Opportunities

—*Anu Kuriakose, Vinshi, P.K.*

Abstract

The transgenders in Kerala have been socially and economically marginalised for a long time. Due to the queer political activism in India and the initiations by the state and central governments, transgenders began to get more visibility in the contemporary times. With the transgender survey and the policy by the government of Kerala, the public sphere started to accommodate transgenders in the past three years. However, they still face certain obstacles in coming out and achieve financial security through education and employment. This paper examines the status of transgenders in Kerala as citizens and their employment opportunities at present. Looking at the cases of some renowned transgenders, the paper sets a model for transgender employability and their social upliftment through generating employment opportunities.

Key words: *Transgenders in Kerala, transgender policy, transgender survey, social upliftment, employment opportunities.*

Introduction

With the quality of life and social development among its people, Kerala, is the most advanced state in India. However, the transgender people in Kerala is marginalised and have been facing social discrimination in every grounds like, education, health, employment opportunities, etc. Being unacceptable in the family and society, many of them have migrated to other states in search of social acceptance and livelihood opportunities. The transgenders face physical abuse due to the social stigma. Since they are thrown out from the family, many of those who face gender dysphoria end up in begging and prostitution.

The judgment of the Supreme Court of India (*National Legal Services Authority v. Union of India,* 2014) granted the right to equality and equal protection for transgender persons (TGs) under Articles 14, 15 and 16 of the Indian Constitution by prohibiting discrimination on the ground of gender identity. The judgment directed the Centre and State Governments to grant TGs full legal recognition of their gender identity. This includes granting legal recognition to a person's self identified gender, as male or female or as third gender, treating transgender persons as socially and educationally backward classes of citizens and extending reservations in public education and employment. The government of Kerala conducted a transgender survey and transgender policy was formulated in the year 2015 which was officially released during the International Conference on Gender Equality 2015 (ICGE) in Thiruvananthapuram.

Employment Status of Transgenders in Indian Context

While defining, occupation, K. Delliswararao and C. Hangsing (2018) have stated that the term is associated with social identity which determines the position of an individual in a society. In India, the hijra community has less than 45% workforce due to the low literacy rate and the others are engaged in prostitution as a means of survival (p.12).

The hijra community has been believed to have special powers and the ability to bring luck. During the Mughal period, eunuchs played an important role in the court administration as royal guards. One such example is the Nizams of Hyderabad who employed a honoured hijra. The sixth Nizam Mahaboob Ali Pasha appointed hijras as confidantes and advisors. Hyderabad state had an Inspector for hijras in the Police Deparrtment (Krishna, Hari Gopala: Sathyajit Gupta, 2002). For centuries, they have performed *badhai*, or blessings at weddings and births. During the British colonial period, their position was deteriorated. After the introduction of Section 377 of IPC transgenders began to be criminalised the resistance movement got recognition which enabled them to fight for their rights and freedom in the post Independent India.

While looking at transgenders in Kerala and the transgender community in other states in India in terms of their employment and livelihood at present, the differences are very much evident. It is believed according to the ancient myths that the hijras "sacrifice their male genitals in return for spiritual power to bless and curse the newlywed and the newborn" (Hossain, 2017, p. 3). As a result of which, the community has been performing at weddings and the birth of children in northern states of India where they have been given certain divinity during the rituals. But most of the time the male-bodied feminine identified transgenders have been functioning as sex workers for their livelihood. The transgender community in the northern states of India traditionally finds their livelihood through begging and prostitution. Yet working as a eunuch earns them stigma and violence on their bodies and the police brutality. When third gender identities are legally recognised and citizenship rights are offered to transgenders in the South Asian region, many have begun to come out openly admitting their gender non-conformity.

Employment Status of Transgenders in Kerala

The survey conducted by the Social Justice Department of Kerala (2014-15) to analyze the social and personal life of transgenders in Kerala found that among the transgenders in the state, "100% of them have had at least one experience of being denied job due to their gender identity" (p. 6). The transgender policy document which was formulated based on the survey, ensures the right to employment for transgenders among many other rights. It recommends that self employment grants must be made available to TG to initiate activities related to raise incomes as well as TG interests. Workplaces/ offices in public and private sector need to sensitise employers and employees on the issue of TG. Anti-discrimination policies must be instituted and meaningfully implemented in the processes of hiring, retention, promotion and employee benefit schemes. Workplace sexual harassment policies should be made TG inclusive. The responsibility is entrusted on Dept. of Labour and Dept. of Industries.

The universal declaration of human rights asserts the right of individuals to work in a job of their choice and to receive equal pay for equal work, without discrimination. Transgenders are often denied this basic human right and tend to be concentrated in low paid temporary jobs. Economic growth is a fundamental requirement for the development of a community in a society. The chart given below shows that only 14% of respondents have permanent work, half are temporarily employed while 6% of respondents work part-time.

According to the survey report on employment proportion, over half of the transgenders have no secure jobs. 23% are employed in private sector and 21% are daily wage labourers.

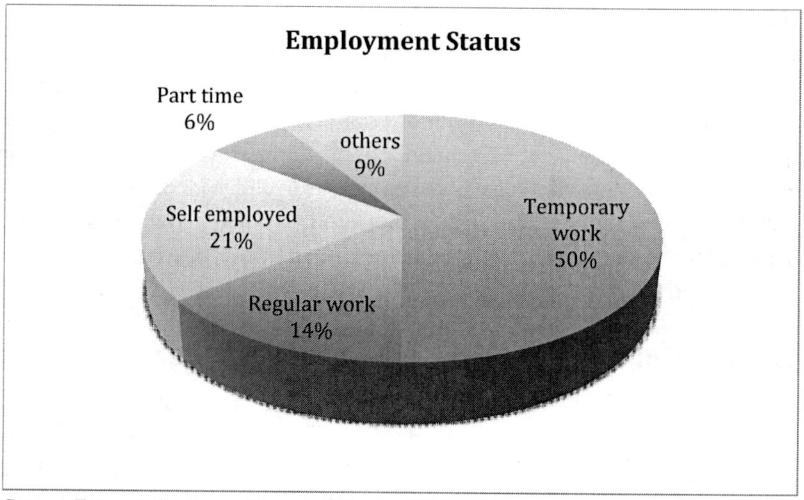

Source: Transgender Survey Report of Kerala, 2014-2015.

Types of workplace discrimination faced by transgenders

Transgender people face severe discrimination in the workplace based on their gender, sexual identity and gender expression. It causes an undue hardship and mental stress for transgenders. Transgender survey of Kerala reveals that transgender or gender non-conforming identity is the main reason for denying jobs for the community.

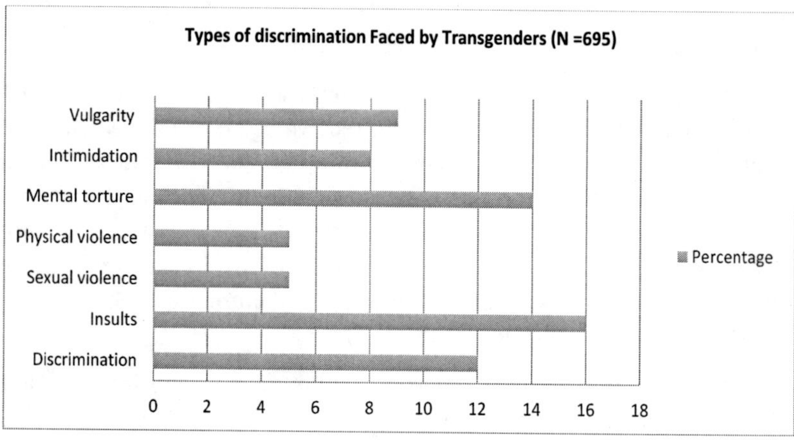

Source: Transgender Survey Report of Kerala, 2014-2015.

The above graph shows that transgenders face different types of violence in employment sector. Insulting and mental torture are severe in this community.

The Government initiatives for mainstreaming transgenders through employment opportunities

The desire for jobs which have dignity and the mainstreaming of transgender identities through employment seek to remove the stigma attached to them in Kerala in the contemporary times. In the past, transgenders in Kerala have migrated to cities in other states and joined the hijra community for home and to live in their transgender identity. The transgender survey held in Kerala points at the employability and opportunities of employment for transgenders in the state who wish to come back. The initiations from the government and the political activism in contemporary Kerala necessitate the need for recognising transgender identity in Kerala by giving them respectable job and livelihood, hence transgenders in the state have offered to be placed in the Kochi Metro project (*The Hindustan Times,* 2017). Around 23 transgenders were hired by the Kochi metro. As the move was widely publicised media applauded the organisation and the Kerala government as socially conscious employers (Nidheesh, 2017). However, many of the transgender employees could not find life smoother with the assured income (10,000 a month for the ticketing staff, 9000 for the housekeeping staff). As reported by *Live Mint*, most of the transgenders employed in the Kochi metro are still to be accepted in the family. The job could not bring significant life change in terms of income, and they struggle to live a normal life.

Gender Taxi is another Kerala government initiative to provide a better means for livelihood for the transgender minority group and to ensure them non-discriminatory treatment in the society. Gender taxi is owned and operated by transgenders. It is an "equality taxi" in which all travellers, irrespective of their gender can avail service. Aimed at elevating the status of transgender community by helping them to become self-employed and independent Kerala government started a "Trans Welfare Co-operative Society".

Case studies

The coming section discusses about transgender people in Kerala, who have had their share of struggle and then rose to inspire people for their employment and social status to achieve recognition in the society.

1. **Renju Renjimar:-** It is to be noted that certain Malayali transgenders have been working as professional makeup artists-for Renju Renjimar (MtF) who work in the entertainment field is acclaimed as Kerala's first 'celebrity bridal' transgender makeup artist with an exceptional and unique style and has reached

audiences in a range of mediums from magazine cover to feature films. Renju has been working as a professional makeup artist for the past 17 years and the makeup he has done for a celebrity has made her famous in the field as a celebrity makeup artist. Renju's profile gave her 'dignity' and respect in the society irrespective of the gender identity Renju has and it is distinguished from the social discrimination other transgenders are facing, and Renju has been set as an example of mainstreaming.

2. **Zara Sheik:-** The first MtF transgender who is placed in IT field in Kerala is Zara Sheik (*News 18 Kerala* 2018). The 27 year old MtF transgender became the first ever transgender person in the state of Kerala to acquire a job in a multinational company. As a BSc Botany graduate Zara took up several jobs in Chennai and Abudabi at the Human Resources departments of different companies as male. However, after returning to Kerala, Zara qualified the three rounds of interviews at UST Global and got a job there. To quote Zara in a newspaper interview,

   > "The company was ready to offer me a job accepting my transgender status. It was my colleagues' behaviour that surprised me. When I went to the office the first day, I had a sinking feeling as to how others would look at me. Breaking all those preconceived notions, they were happy to accommodate me and they all respected my identity. The company also informed me that I could use the ladies washroom and toilets, which according to me is a great acceptance".

   The experience of Zara Sheik at a multinational company in Kerala brings out the transformation happens in Kerala in terms of employment opportunities. The transgender policy document assures employment opportunities for transgenders and the welcome attitude that Zara received from the company where she joined, should be assured to every persons who want to secure job with their transgender identities.

3. **Tripthi Shetty:-** Tripthi Shetty, another Malayali MtF transgender now acclaimed as a transgender activist, entrepreneur, has received the artisan card from the central governments' the Ministry of Textiles and she has been a transgender model by profession. It is the first time that a transgender has received such recognition from the government. Tripthi, an MtF sees the recognition as gift for the entire transgender community in India, as she can participate

in all exhibitions conducted in India. Tripthi Shetty has given the social acceptance through the respectable job opportunity. Rather than involving in the sex trade, she chose to be different and has set an example for the members of the transgender community.

4. **Deepthi Nair:-** Deepthi Nair, an MtF transgender has created history by becoming the cover girl of *Vanitha*, a leading women's magazine in Malayalam besides being a famous MtF transgender model (*India Today* 2016). Becoming a 'cover girl' gave Deepthi the social acceptance; her family members agreed her identity and she began to get offers from fashion field.

   Many other transgenders like Syama S. Prabha, Sheethal Syam, Vihaan Pithamber, Vineeth Seema etc. are figures celebrated by the media for their achievements as transgenders and transgender activists. Thus, it is observed that transgenders in Kerala are coming out from the shackles, from prostitution and begging, which have been emblematic of the hijra community in North Indian states which has stigmatized them as social outcasts for a long time. The example set by government initiatives like the Kochi metro, transgender cell, transgender justice board and space in educational institutions are also significant at this point. However employability should reach to all those members who are marginalised due to lack of education and low social status.

Conclusion

The right to livelihood is a part of the right to life and transgenders should not be discriminated against getting an opportunity to a dignified job in government or private sectors as the citizens of India. Job security should be accompanied by a cordial environment and for that the mindset of the employers and the society as a whole should be changed. The state public service commission under the aegis of the government of Kerala should ensure that transgenders are also treated as par with cisgender candidates. Kerala government has stood with them through its various policies and programmes the transgender community still has a long way to go towards gender equality. The following observations are recommended to bring a change in the employment sector for transgenders.

Recommendations

- Conduct literacy and skill development programmes for transgenders.
- Start special vocational courses like tailoring, beautician, toy making etc for transgenders.

- Provide financial support and loan for starting self enterprises.
- Provide leadership training.
- Open up the existing Social Welfare Schemes for transgenders and create specific welfare schemes to address the basic needs of transgenders including housing and employment needs.

Work cited

1. Hossain, A. (2017). The paradox of recognition: hijra, third gender and sexual rights in Bangladesh. *Culture, health & sexuality*, *19*(12), 1418-1431.
2. Konduru, D., & Hangsing, C. Socio–Cultural Exclusion and Inclusion of Transgenders in India. *International Journal of Social Sciences and Management*, *5*(1), 10-17.
3. Krishna, Hari Gopala; Satyajit Gupta. (2002). *The Twilight Zone of Transsexuals.* Combat Law.
4. Priya Lekshmi. (12 February 2018) "In a First, Kerala To Set Up Co-Operative Societies for Transgenders." https://www.thebetterindia.com/130814/kerala-transgender-community-co-operative-societies/
5. Social Justice Department of Kerala (2015), *State Policy for Transgenders in Kerala 2015.*Thiruvanathapuram.
6. Social Justice Department of Kerala (2015), *Transgender Survey Report 2014-2015.*
7. Sudhish, Navamy (11 January 2015), "The Aphrodite touch Renju Renjimar most sought after make-up artist," *Indian Express.*
8. Think Change India. (30 May 2017). "Meet Zara Sheikha, the first transgender person from Kerala to get a job in an MNC". *Yourstory.com.* https://yourstory.com/2017/05/zara-sheikha-transgender-kerala/
9. Think Change India. (2017 February 5), "After She-Taxi, Kerala to launch G-Taxi for transgenders". https://yourstory.com/2016/02/kerala-g-taxi-transgenders/
10. TNN. (2018, January 6). "Transgender person gets artisan ID from Handicrafts Corporation." *The Times of India.* https://timesofindia.indiatimes.com/city/kochi/transgender-person-gets-artisan-id-from- handicrafts-corporation/articleshow/62390001.cms

12

From Discrimination to Accommodation: The Need to Promote Transgender Awareness in Society

— *Dr. Thomas Joseph*

Introduction

Transgenders are often considered as one of the most marginalised groups in a social order. As the transgender population has become more visible in many countries in the recent years, there has been increased research concerning transgenders and their living conditions. Inspite of all constitutional guarantees, the transgender community is denied even their basic rights, which include Freedom of Expression, Right Against Violence, Right to Personal Liberty, Dignity, Right to Education and Empowerment, Right Against Discrimination and Exploitation.

This paper is an attempt to dwell on the acute discrimination faced by this community and the possible ways to free them from this unjust order and to integrate them to the mainstream of the society.

Who is a Transgender ?

The term 'Transgender' is an umbrella term that includes transsexuals, transvestites, intersexual people, and just about anybody else who doesn't confirm to the traditional model of sex/gender. Transgender is the most general, inclusive term. Generally speaking, the term transgender refers to people who deviate from the heteronormative order. Typically, a transgender person is someone whose sense of gender is different from their physical characteristics or the sex assigned to him/her at the time of birth. According to World Health Organisation, transgender is an umbrella term for people whose gender identity and expression does not conform to the norms and expectations traditionally associated with the sex assigned to them at birth. It includes people who are transsexual, transgender or otherwise considered gender non-conforming. Transgender is both male and female to male (F+M) and for female (M+F) gender transgressions.

'Trans' is often used as shorthand for transgender. In India, the transgenders are now-a-days considered to be the 'Third Gender'. Trans individuals might feel they belong to the other gender, i.e., transwomen, transmen, and therefore have a binary concept of gender. They might feel they belong to both or neither genders recognised by the mainstream society, and thus have a non-binary concept of gender. The transgenders fall under the category of LGBTQ group. The LGBTQ group is referred to as the Lesbian, gay, bisexual, transgender, and Queer community which includes those with gender dysphoria and different sexual orientations. The Lesbian and gay people have been accepted in many parts of world and have also got their rights, but the transgender is still without rights.

Historical Perspective of Transgenders

There are references to transgender persons and communities in ancient civilisations of trans and in classical writings. India's transgender community has been a part of the subcontinent from time immemorial. They have a recorded history of over 4000 years. They are mentioned in ancient literature. The concept of Napumsaka had been on integral part of the Hindu mythology folklore, epic and early Vedic and Puranic literature. The best known of which is the Kama Sutra, an ancient text on human sexual behaviour written sometime between 400 BCE and 200 CE. Hijra characters hold significant roles in some of the most important texts of Vedic period and other early literature, including the Mahabharata and the Ramayana. One of the many forms of Siva, a principal Hindu deity, involves him merging with his wife, Parvati, to become the androgynous Ardhanari, who holds special significance to many in the Hijra Community. The earlier Tamil Grammar Tolkappiyam (3rd century BC) also refers to hermaphrodite as a third 'neuter' gender.

In the pre-colonial period, Hijras enjoyed dignified status. Hijras played prominent role in the royal court of Islamic world particularly in the Ottoman empire and the Mugal rule in Medieval India. They enjoyed influential position and have been considered as one of the important figures in the society. The Mugals entrusted the Hijras with the responsibility of protecting their women and children. They also played well-known positions as political advisors and administrators. They were considered as clever, trustworthy, loyal and had free access to all. The sixth Nizam Mahboob Ali Pasha employed hijras as confidantes and advisors, domestic supervisors and menial domestics. They also occupied their positions in the Islamic religious institutions especially in guarding the Holy places of Mecca and Medina. They enjoyed a life of privilege and proximity to the royalty. For countries, they have performed *badhai*, or blessings at weddings and births.

With the advent of the British rule in the 18th century, there was a gradual downfall in the status and acceptance of transgenders in the public space. The transgender presence in the public sphere was seen as deviance in the colonial space. The British administration vigorously criminalised the Hijras community and to denied them the civil rights. The disgusted colonists passed a law in 1897 classifying all transgenders as criminals. British authorities sought to eradicate and criminalise the Hijra community through various laws. As a result, they remained stigmatized and marginalised. They were considered to be separate tribes in different parts of India by the colonial administration. Now, the transgender persons are continuously facing multiple forms of social decimation and oppression in the country. Now they are an ignored segment of the society and face deep and pervasive discriminations. Despite protection under various provisions of the Constitution.

Exclusion from All Spheres

According to the Indian Census of 2011, 4,87,803 lakhs have been classified as transgender out of which 54854 is below 6 years. The highest proportion of the third gender population, about 28% was identified in Uttar Pradesh followed by 9% in Andhra Pradesh, 8% each in Maharashtra and Bihar, over 6% in both Madhya Pradesh and West Bengal and well over 4% in Tamil Nadu, Karnataka and Odisha. Rajasthan accounted for over 3% of the total transgender population and Punjab for 2%.The issue of transgender is still in debate and uncertain even after the Supreme Court of India recognised them as a third gender people.

Transgender people encounter many challenges. They face discrimination, different treatment, and undue attention in their each and every phase of life. Transgender people experience discrimination because of their gender identity and gender expression, and may also experience segregation because of their sexual orientation or perceived sexual orientation.

Transgender people are often the victims of abuse and prejudice. They are thrown out from their families and ostracised in society and state.

Their own relatives hide them to cover the so-called 'shame'. Sometimes, the child or teenager may decide to run away from the family not able to tolerate the discrimination or not wanting to bring shame to ones family. When they are rejected and pushed out of their family, they are forced to run away in search of a livelihood, home and community that befit their sexual identity.

Transgender people experience extensive stigma and discrimination and suffer mental ill health. They are facing a lot of barriers in public places, such as, restaurants, parks, hotels, libraries, movies, theaters, shopping malls etc. They experience pervasive discrimination at work also. Schools and colleges are difficult places for transgender students is they regularly face humiliation. The harassment and the resultant mental trauma have a cumulative negative effect on their personality. They also face social and physical abuse which may lead to some physiological disorder problem. They are been thrown from their own family and villages which give them no option but to engage themselves as sexworkers or as beggars in the street. Some members of the society ridicule gender-variant people for being different and they may even be hostile. The government of India introduced many welfare policies and schemes to improve the socio-economic conditions and constitutional safeguards for the transgender people.

Third Gender in Current Scenario

Everyone has the right to be recognised as a dignified person before the law. In a path-breaking judgement, the Supreme Court has affirmed the constitutional rights and freedom of third gender persons.

The Supreme Court of India passed a unique judgement in April 2014, stating one's sexual orientation as the integral part of personality, dignity and freedom and identified transgender as a third gender. In 2014, the Rajya Sabha passed the Rights of Transgender Bill and in 2015, the government passed another Bill, Rights for Transgender Persons Bill. The 2015 Bill underwent further changes and another Bill was introduced in the Lok Sabha in 2016. The Transgender persons (Protection of Rights Bill). This inspired hope amongst the members of this community and among their supporters. The Bill met with criticism and protests from Indian transgender persons and was referred to the standing committee, which submitted its report in July 2018. The Lok Sabha tabled and passed a newer version of the Bill with twenty-seven amendments on 17 December 2018. The Bill was reintroduced in 19 July 2019 by the Minister of Social Justice and

Empowerment, Thawar Chand Gehlot. The Bill was passed by the Rajya Sabha on 26th November, 2019 and already passed by the 17th Lok Sabha on 5th August 2019 as Transgender Persons (Protection of Rights) Act, 2019. The main highlights of the Bill are:

(1) The Bill defines a transgender person as one whose gender does not match the gender assigned at birth. It includes trans-men and trans-women, persons with intersex variations, gender-queers and persons with socio-cultural identities, such as kinnar and hijra.

(2) A transgender person must obtain a certificate of identity as proof of recognition of identity as transgender and to confer upon them right to self-perceived gender identity.

(3) Such a certificate would be granted by the District Magistrate on the recommendation of a screening officer, a government official, and a transgender person.

(4) The Bill prohibits discrimination against a transgender person in areas such as education, employment, and healthcare. It directs the central and state government to provide Welfare Schemes in these areas.

(5) Every transgender person shall have a right to be reside and be included in his household.

(6) Offences such as compelling a transgender person to beg, denial of access to a public place, physical and sexual abuse etc, would attract up to 2 years of imprisonment and a penalty.

The Bill will benefit a large number of transgender persons to mitigate the stigma, discrimination and abuse against this marginalised section and bring them in to the mainstream of society. It will lead to greater inclusiveness and will make the transgenders productive and proactive members of the society.

Conclusion

Transgender people have a gender identity that is different from the sex that they were assigned at birth. Being trans is part of the rich diversity of human nature. Being different should not be treated as a disorder. To treat a transgender person with respect, you treat them according to their gender identity, not their sex at birth. They have a right to human dignity. They are part and parcel of the social order and they have equal rights in everything. Acceptance by society itself will help to some extend to get them decent living space. The society and their own families in particular should accept them as they are. Therefore, it is imperative to educate all groups of people about the rights of the transgenders and the need to integrate them into the mainstream of the society. Sincere attention and intervention of Government and NGOs would certainly bring positive outcome towards this end. Awareness programme and conscientisation campaigns for the members of the society need to be carried out in order to ensure the social inclusion of the transgenders. Institutions should create a safe and non-discriminatory environment for the welfare of the third gender.

References

1. Dutt, N. Eunuch – India's Third Gender, Things Asian, The Diplomat, 2012.
2. Kimmel. *The Gendered Society*, New York: Oxford, 2004.
3. Michelraj, M. Historical Evolution of Transgender Community in India, *Asian Rev Soc SCI,* 2015.
4. Nanda, S. *Neither Man Nor Women: The Hijras of India,* Belmount, C A: Wads Worth Publishing, 1990.
5. Nanda, S. The gender Diversity: Cross-Cultural Variations, Waveland Press, 2000.
6. Saxena, P., *Life of a Eunuch,* Santa Publishing House, 2011.
7. Government of India Census, 2011 (online), Available: httpp:// www.census2011.co.in/transgender.php

13

Legal Measures for the Protection of the Rights of the Transgender Community: A Study of Transgender Persons (Protection of Rights) Act, 2019

— *Soumya, S*

Introduction

Transgender community has been actively occupying the socio-economic and political space for the past several years. This has been attributed to a number of reasons such as the intervention from governments including legal measures, increasing recognition of sexual identities by various societies etc. In family space also, there has been tremendous support for the Trans community to express their sexual identity. Albeit such a situation could be manifested in various societies both developing and developed, the socio-economic and political status of the transgender persons is still to be improved. The trans people suffer numerous violations of rights and many of them still turn to prostitution for their livelihood. The educational and employment opportunities are denied to a majority of transgender community. The social practices like marriage and family life is still anathema to the life of transgender persons. In this backdrop, it is significant to look into the various legal measures adopted in India for the protection of the trans people with a particular thrust on the "Transgender Persons (Protection Rights) Act, 2019".

Legal History of Transgender Community in India

The legislative provisions for the protection of transgender community could be traced back to the British period. One of the significant legislative measures in the British period was the Criminal Tribes Act, 1871 intended to prosecute the tribes who were innately criminal and were keen on undertaking non-bailable offences. The provisions which were relevant in the act for transgender persons were registration, surveillance and control of certain criminal tribes and had penalised eunuchs who apparently worn women's dresses and ornaments in public places. Under the law, the eunuchs were denied playing music and dancing in public places. The penalty for such acts was arrest without warrant and imprisonment up to two years or fine or both. However, this act was replaced by Central Legislation i.e. Habitual Offenders Act stressing on targeting individuals rather than criminal tribes. The British authorities perceived transgender or Hijras as a constant threat to colonial authority. There were number of reasons for the hatred of the transgender community as the colonial masters believed that Hijras as "professional sodomites" who pose a challenge to colonial legal system, which was based on heterosexual, reproductive sexuality and the family system. The Criminal Tribes Act was repealed in 1949. However, there were some legislations particularly at the local level which had also penetrated into the lives of the transgender community in various ways. One of the significant legislation at the regional level was the Andhra Pradesh (Telangana Area) Eunuchs Act 1329F. It was renamed by the Telangana Eunuchs Act. The Section 4 of the Act instructs that transgender persons could be arrested without a warrant if they found to be in female clothing or performing in public places. Similarly the Karnataka Police Act of 1963 also had provisions of monitoring and imposing criminality among 'eunuchs'.

Section 377 of Indian Penal Code (IPC) yet another measure from the British regime. It intends to criminalise non-vaginal sexual acts between individuals encompassing anal and oral sex. Even the Supreme Court had also criminalised sexual penetration other than the heterosexual penile-vaginal. Section 377 is an anti-sodomy provision. The following excerpts from Section 377 indicates the draconian aspect.

> 377. Unnatural offences. — Whoever voluntarily has carnal intercourse against the order of nature with any man, woman, or animal, shall be punished with[1] (imprisonment for life), or with imprisonment of either description for a term which may extend to ten years, and shall be liable to fine. Explanation. — Penetration is sufficient to constitute the carnal intercourse necessary to the offence described in this section.

In 2018, the Supreme Court repealed section 377 of the Indian Penal code and the Court had taken the position that "the sexual orientation of an individual is natural and discrimination on the basis of sexual orientation is a violation of freedom of expression. The LGBT community has the same rights as any ordinary citizen..... Criminalising gay sex is irrational and indefensible. The provision of IPC had resulted in collateral effect in that consensual sex between LBBTQ people is criminalised and is violation of Article 14". By repealing Section 377, the Highest Court of India observed that the fundamental rights of sexual and gender minorities are protected and declares that the right to life and dignity includes the two dimensions of one's identity and sexual orientation.

Constitutional Safeguards for Transgender Persons

Constitutional protection of transgender community could be manifested in the fundamental rights. Albeit the term 'transgender' is not mentioned in the fundamental rights, the fundamental rights have clearly expressed the notions of inclusiveness through 'sex' and 'any person'. The Right to equality guarantees every citizen equal status and equal protection within the territory of India. Any person mentioned in the Right to equality provision of the fundamental rights encompasses every individual irrespective of caste, religion, sex and other demarcations.

This provision explains the fact that a transgender person is not to be discriminated. *The National Legal Services Authority V. Union of India* judgement had given a wider interpretation of the term 'person' and the term 'person' is not confined to binary manifestations of male or female. Hijras or transgender persons or sexually non-confirming persons are also included in the term 'person'.

Therefore, such kind of sexually non-confirming persons are entitled to all kinds of protection against discriminations of various nature such as socio-political and economic.

Equality of opportunity and right against all kinds of discriminations is another constitutional based right which has provisions for the protection of trans persons. The term 'sex' is significant in this context. Sex is also an all-encompassing term which includes persons whose sex is different from the original sex at the time of his or her birth. The Supreme Court of India has observed that both gender and biological aspects constitute different components of sex. The biological manifestations include genitals, chromosomes, and secondary sexual features. On the other hand, gender indicates intensive psychological and emotional dimensions of sexual identity and character. Article 15(2) and 16 (4) has been subjected to interpretation to impart social equality to transgender community in the nature of equal opportunity in employment. It also stipulates state to make special provisions for the upliftment of trans persons in every walk of life. Complement to the articles in the constitution, the Directive Principles of State Policy also contains the notions of social equality which the transgender persons could claim in their fight against social exclusion.

Article 19(1) (a) is also significant for transgender community as it provides certain basic values such as privacy, self-identity, autonomy, and personal integrity. Right to life is a notable fundamental right since it gives an opportunity for any person to lead a dignified life. Transgender community has every right to live a dignified life. The right to reputation as part of the right to life is meaningful here in the sense that transgender persons are subjected to various kinds of humiliation in the domestic and external realms of societal life.

Right against exploitation is a crucial fundamental right in the sense that it has provisions to prevent inhuman practices such as human trafficking and beggary.

Article 23 of the constitution assimilates these values and sexuality minority groups including the transgender community could take advantage of it. The trans persons are often involved in sexual exploitation, prostitution and various kinds of exploitation.

Legal Protection of Transgender Community

The legal provisions in the form of legislations from time to time evoke a lot of opportunities for the community. The Citizenship Amendment Act, 1955 does not deny a person citizenship on the basis of gender identity. Similarly, the Registration of Births and Deaths Act, 1969 does not have provisions of gender identity for registration of birth or death. The Immoral Traffic Prevention Act, 1956 which was amended in 1986 was significant in terms of prevention trafficking among women and children. By the amendment of the Act 1986, the scope of the act now covers those persons whose gender identity is indeterminable. It led to a situation in which transgender individuals are prevented from falling in to prostitution.

However, despite the legal and constitutional safeguards the socio-economic and political conditions of the community are far from satisfactory. Now the decriminalisation process has been achieved, the next endeavour is to gain positive rights. The positive rights include the right to marry, the right to reservations in education and employment, the right to adopt and have family, inherit property. Right to have access to public places and right not to be discriminated.

Some of the initiatives in such a direction were taken in 2014 in the form of Rights of Transgender Persons Bill. It was proposed as a private members bill. The draft of the proposed Bill was not introduced and later two Bills were initiated by the government. These are Transgender Persons (Protection of Rights) Bills 2016 and 2018. However, these bills were subjected to severe criticism by the transgender community.

These initiatives were not suffice to protect the community from various kinds of discriminations and violence unleashed. The criminal law on sexual molest in India is still gender focused. The victims of sexual violence are referred to as

'women'. The significant laws in the country do not cover trans persons such as Domestic Violence Act, 2005. The transgender persons are increasingly undergoing discriminations even within the family.

Transgender Persons (Protection) Bill 2019: An Evaluation

Historical Context of the Act

In 2013, government formed an expert committee to study the problems of transgender people and recommend guidelines for protection of the community. The committee consisting of experts from various fields had studied the conditions in Tamil Nadu and had recommended several ways by which the issues affecting transgender community could be addressed. The recommendations include designating the nomenclature "third gender" and mitigation of the health maladies of the transgender community.

In 2014, a private member bill the Rights of Transgender People was introduced in Rajya Sabha by Tiruchi Siva, a Member of Parliament form Tamil Nadu, which had looked into a range of entitlements of such persons, providing specifically for them in health, skill development and employment opportunities and protection from abuse and torture education sectors. The bill was passed by Rajya Sabha. The bill could not materialise owing to the dissolution of sixteenth Lok Sabha and lapsed.

In 2016, the government introduced its own bill in the Lok Sabha . It was referred to the Standing Committee which recommended intersex person's rights, granting reservations for socially and economically backward persons and recognition of civil rights such as marriage, partnership, divorce and adoption.

The Transgender Persons (Protection of Rights) Bill 2019 has been passed by the Parliament. The Bill was passed by the Rajya Sabha on

26th November, 2019 and already passed by the 17th Lok Sabha on 5th August, 2019. The Bill has following provisions:

(i) Non-discrimination against a Transgender person in educational institutions, employment, employment and healthcare services etc.

(ii) Recognition of identity of Transgender Persons and to confer up on them right to self-perceived gender identity.

(iii) Provision of right of residence with parents and immediate family members.

(iv) Provision for formulation of welfare schemes and programmes for education, social security and health of transgender persons.

(v) Provision for National Council for Transgender Persons to advice, monitor and evaluate measures for the protection of their rights.

Definition of Transgender

The Bill defines a transgender person as one whose gender does not confirm with gender assigned at birth. According to the Bill, Transgender is an umbrella term which includes trans-men and trans-women, persons with intersex variations, gender- queers, and persons with socio-cultural identities such as kinnar and hijra. Intersex person is a person who are by birth manifests variations in his or her primary sexual features, external genitalia, chromosomes or hormones form the normative standard of male or female body.

The Bill in its comprehensive form encompasses the following provisions:-

- **Prohibition against discrimination**

  The Bill has provisions which prohibits the discrimination against a transgender person, including denial of service or unfair treatment in connection with: (i) Education; (ii) employment; (iii) healthcare; (iv) access to, or enjoyment of goods, facilities, opportunities available to the public; (v) right to movement; (vi) right to reside, rent, or otherwise occupy property; (vii) opportunity to hold public or private office; and (viii) access to a government or private establishment in whose care or custody a transgender person is.

- **Right of residence**

  Every transgender person is entitled to reside and be included in his household. In case the immediate family member is unable to take care of the transgender person, the person may be placed in a rehabilitation centre, on the orders of a competent court.

- **Employment**

  No government or private entity can discriminate against a transgender person in employment issues, including recruitment, and promotion. Every establishment is required to designate a person to be complaint officer to deal with complaints to the Act.

- **Education**

  Educational institutions funded or recognised by the relevant government shall provide inclusive education, sports, and recreational facilities for transgender persons without discrimination.

- **Healthcare**

  The government shall initiate steps to provide health facilities to transgender persons including separate HIV surveillance centres, and sex reassignment surgeries. The government shall review medical curriculum to address health issues of transgender persons, and provide comprehensive medical insurance schemes for them.

- **Conflict of identity for a transgender person**

  A transgender person could make an application to the District Magistrate for a certificate of identity, indicating the gender as 'transgender'. A revised certificate may be obtained only if the individual undergoes surgery to change their gender either as a male or a female.

- **Welfare measures by the government**

  The Bill states that the relevant government will take measures to ensure the full inclusion and participation of transgender persons in society. It must also take steps for their rescue and rehabilitation, vocational training and self-employment, create schemes that are transgender sensitive, and promote their participation in cultural activities.

- **Offences and penalties**

  The Bill recognises the following offences against transgender persons: (i) forced or bonded labour (excluding compulsory government service for public purposes), (ii) denial of use of public places, (iii) removal from household, and village,

(iv) physical, sexual, verbal, emotional or economic abuse. Penalties for these offences vary between six months and two years, and a fine.

- **National Council for Transgender Persons (NCT)**

  The NCT will comprise of: (i) Union Minister for Social Justice (Chair Person); (ii) Minister of State for Social Justice (Vice-Chairperson); (iii) Secretary of the Ministry of Social Justice; (iv) one representative from ministries including Health, Home Affairs, and Human Resources Development. Other members include representatives of NITI Ayog, and the National Human Rights Commission. State government will also be represented. The Council will also consist of five members from the transgender community and five experts from non-governmental organisations.
- The Council will advise the central government as well as monitor the impact of policies, legislation and projects with respect to transgender persons. It will also address the grievances of transgender persons.

Responses and Reactions to the Act

The Transgender Persons (Protection of Rights) Bill, 2019 had evoked much criticism even before it was passed by the Lok Sabha. The human rights organisations have raised much apprehensions about the bill. One of the vibrant human rights organisations Human Rights Watch argued that the proposed bill was unclear on a transgender person's right to self-identify, which the Apex Court had recognised in a landmark judgement in 2014. The Transgender Persons Bill has inclusive provisions on " transgender persons" and a well-defined demarcation between identity based recognition of and medical procedures some transgender persons desire. The Human Rights Watch contends that albeit the bill has provisions for the transgender persons to express their self-perceived gender identity, it can be interpreted to mean that transgender people are forced to have certain surgeries before legally changing their gender. Meenakshi Ganguly, the South Asian Director of Human Rights Watch is critical of the bill and argues that "the transgender Persons Bill should be a remarkable achievement for a long persecuted community, but the current draft fails on the fundamental right to self-identify".

The bill according to the organisation seems to make it compulsory two-step process for legal gender recognition. The first procedure requires the transgender person to apply for a "transgender certificate". This can be done on the basis of a person's self-declared identity. Then, the certificate holder could apply for "change in gender certificate", which gives an indication to authorities to change their legal gender to male or female. The second process is to undergo surgery and then by documentation by a medical authority confirming it.

The proposed bill empowers the district magistrate to judge the "validity" of the application and decide whether to issue the change in gender certificate but does not provide guidelines on how this decision should be made. The Human Rights Watch further contends that the bill is conspicuous by its absence on whether a trans person who is in possession of male or female gender certificate will have access to government welfare schemes and programmes meant for transgender people.

Apart from the apparent violations of the apex court verdict, ambiguity regarding the manifestation of transgender person's identity is contradictory to international standards for gender recognition. The various international standards and best practices such as United Nations agencies, the World Medical Association and the World Professional Association for transgender health recommend demarcation of legal and medical processes of gender reassignment for transgender people. The recommendations involves the removal of evaluations of applicants for legal gender recognition by a group of psychologists, physicians, or other experts. It is also recommended that self-declared identity form the basis of utilising all security measures, benefits, and entitlements.

The UN Office of the High Commissioner for Human Rights in 2015 had reaffirmed that states had to take immediate steps "issuing legal identity documents, upon request, that reflect preferred gender, eliminating abusive preconditions, such as sterilisations, forced treatment and divorce". In 2015, report published by the World Health Organisation and the Asia-Pacific Transgender Network suggested that governments "take all necessary legislative, administrative and other measures to fully recognise each person's self-defined gender identity, with no medical requirements or discrimination on any grounds.

However, it is significant to include the term intersex persons in the bill and the bill is to be renamed the Rights of Transgender and Intersex Persons Bill.

It is also mandatory to include in the bill consent of intersex individuals before non-emergency surgical procedures are conducted and prevent medically unnecessary procedures on children. Intersex persons may be issued legal identity documents that manifest their gender and the government should make sure that intersex persons and organisations are consulted with regard to laws and policies that have implications on their rights.

Besides, the bill should have provisions to train teachers to help them adopt inclusive teaching methods to ensure transgender students are not harassed or discriminated against by teaching community and other children.

The term “family” in the act was questioned by many civil society organisations. The “family” nomenclature brings a meaningless entity to many transgender persons as most of the community living not living with their biological family and their immediate neighbourhood. It is in the family they encounter violence and discrimination. It is also alleged that the act is a toothless tiger because the provision for prohibiting discrimination has certain shortcomings such as lack of an enforcing authority, lack of medical measures in terms of compensation or any other measures for the victim and lack of punitive action against the violator. The transgender community is also apprehensive about the ‘rescue, protection and rehabilitation’ measures in the act as it brings back the bitter memories of shelter homes.

Another grey area in the act is the responsibilities of the complaint officer. The process of selecting a complaint officer is not clearly defined.

The healthcare issues of the trans persons mentioned in the act is not satisfactory as well as alleged by certain organisations. They blame that there is not a single organised protocol guiding the medical community with regard to the healthcare of the transgender community. The primary health centres have to be transgender sensitive in the sense that their fertility, artificial fertilisation and surrogacy are to be taken care of. The mental health of the transgender persons are also to be addressed.

The National Council for Transgender persons is constrained for lack of autonomy. The National Council which is composed by 30 persons has a meagre representation of five persons from the transgender community.

Albeit the Transgender persons Bill has provisions criminalising begging and sex work, it has brought about a new section that criminalises ‘compelling or enticing’ a transgender person to indulge in forced labour. The new addition seems to be redundant as there is a pre-existing “Bonded Labour System (Abolition) Act” which is authorised to penalise those persons employing bonded labour and is applicable to persons with no discrimination on gender. Some of the punitive measures against perpetrators of violence against trans persons are repetitive in nature without any changes from previous drafts.

The Constitutional Challenge of the Transgender Act

The act was challenged before the Supreme Court, by Assam's first trans judge Swati Bidhan Baruah. The challenge could be categorised into – the self-determination challenge (Article 21), the equality challenge (Article 14), the non-discrimination challenge (Article 14), the affirmative action challenge (Article 16) and the positive obligations challenge (Article 21).

The Self-Determination Challenge

The petition challenges Sections 4 to 6 of the transgender act on the basis that producing self-identification "subject to certification by state" is unconstitutional. The basis of this allegation is rooted on two judgements of the Supreme Court: *NALSA v Union of India and Puttaswamy (I) v Union of India*. In NALSA, Supreme Court gave the verdict that the right to gender identity was safeguarded under Articles 19 and 21 of the Constitution. In the case of Puttaswamy the court held that the right to privacy protected the freedom to take intimate decisions that allowed minimum interference from the state. The petitions contends that the certification violates both the rulings. The petitions challenges Section 7 of the act which indicates that once a certificate of identity is issued and in the context of a transgender person wants to change their gender, it can be permissible only on a submission of a certificate by the Chief Medical Officer of the institution where the applicant has undergone surgery.

The Equality Challenge

The Sections 4 to 7 are also challenged in the sense that they violate the right to equality. The first argument is that the act imposes burdens up on transgender individuals (certification) than on non-trans persons. However, this challenge is not significant as the accepted norm is cisgender and transgender is the "exception".

The Non-Discrimination Challenge

Section 3 of the Act provides that non-discrimination issues where it prohibits discrimination against transgender individuals in various sectors such as provision of services, education, housing etc. However, the Act does not provide no penalty or remedy for violation of these provisions.

The petition rightly pointed out that a right without a remedy is worthless and indeed, is not a right at all.

Another challenge in this context is Section 18 of the Act which recommends punishment of up to two years imprisonment for a series of offences against transgender individuals such as forced labour, denial of access to public spaces, abuse and so on. The petition argues that similar offences in other contexts such as bonded labour in general or rape invite much more stringent penalties. As the transgender community is already marginalised and vulnerable to various forms of violence and abuse, it is necessary to make penalties more harsh and rigorous.

The Affirmative Action Challenge

The NALSA and Supreme Court have affirmed that transgender community was to be treated as "socially and educationally backward class" for the purpose of availing of reservation schemes under Articles 15 and 16 of the Constitution. The Act never mentions about the affirmative action.

Conclusion

The history of transgender community's fight for social justice has ups and downs. The British government promulgated various legislations and such legal measures perceived the community as a constant threat to colonial regime. Section 377 of the Indian Penal Code was a draconic law which did not bother to accept the gender identity and emotions of not only transgender community but also to the whole LGBTQ community. The Constitution has ensured the protection of human rights of the transgender community through the provision of fundamental rights. Albeit, the inclusion of fundamental rights in our constitution the transgender people are marginalised in a big manner. It was in this context that government had initiated two bills for the protection of transgender community. The bills were introduced in 2016 and 2018. These bills were not satisfactory in addressing the woes of the community. In 2019, that government has introduced The Transgender Persons (Protection of Rights) Bill which was expected to uplift the status of the trans people. The promulgation of the bill had met with severe criticism from the community and civil society organisations. The major criticism levelled against the Act is the question of identity of the transgender people. The identity needs to be approved by a competent authority of the state. Similar kind of shortcomings are raised against the Act by various sections of the society. The shortcomings and vulnerabilities of Act are to be addressed by the government as the transgender community is struggling to make their vibrant presence in the Indian society.

References

Decoding Section 377. What it means for the LGBTQ Community-Your story retrieved from https://your story.com

Gautam Bhatia, (n.d).The Constitutional Challenge to the Transgender Act retrieved from http://indconlawphil.wordspress.com

India: Transgender Bill Raises Rights Concerns retrieved from https://www.hrw.org

Kothari, (n.d). Section 377 and Beyond retrieved from https://clpr.org.in

Justin Jos (2017). Limiting Gender Variance: Critical Reflections on Transgender Persons Bill, Economic and Political Weekly LII(4): 21,28 January.

Rachana Mudraboyina,(n.d). A Critique of Transgender Persons (Protection of Rights) Bill, 2019 retrieved from http://feminisminindia.com

Remya Kannan (2019). Why are there objections to the Transgender Persons Bill? Retrieved from the hindu.com/news/national/

The Transgender Persons (Protection of Rights) Bill, 2019 retrieved from https://www.prsindia.org

14

Mainstreaming Gender in Governance: From Women Empowerment to Gender Equality

— ***Parvathy, N.S.***

Abstract

Around the world, Gender and Governance are the two terms which hardly comes together. Though the case of Kerala is not much different, its Transgender policy, 2015 was a milestone in discourses on Gender Governance. The radicalism of this policy was much acclaimed by the media around the world. But the question persists that whether Kerala is that Gender sensitive to accommodate its propositions? Or this policy too be dusted once its media hype is over? In order to predict the trend, let us do a review of recent policy initiatives of Kerala on Gender empowerment. Though the Gender and Development statistics of Kerala are better than other regions in the country, its policies exclusively focusing on women empowerment failed miserably to reach the objective of Gender equality. The concept of Gender Mainstreaming introduced as a new theoretical tool to compensate.The Gender Equality and Women's EmpowermentGEWE policy, 2015 was first policy document that talked about the potential of Gender mainstreaming. Gender manual of 2015 shows the institutional efforts for the process of Gender mainstreaming. Celebrated policies like ***Gender Park, She taxi, She stay, SadhairyamMunnottu*** *were conceived and executed. Unfortunately, many of such innovative ideas have an episodic existence. Failure or ineffectiveness of these policies emphasises that conscientious efforts aiming eradication of Gender dogmas and Homophobia can only make significant impacts while addressing Gender inequality.*

The term 'Gender' indicates the socially constructed roles and responsibilities which are recognised as suitable for men and women. Gender equality means that men and women should have equal power and prospects for education, financial independence and personal development. Gender equality is globally accepted as an essential human right. Even though the world is making progress in achieving gender parity, a huge discrepancy exists between men and women in the areas of health, education, political power and economic resources. Women have fewer opportunities for economic participation than men, less access to basic and higher education, greater health and safety risks, and less political representation. Solving this gender gap through women empowerment is an important step in achieving gender equality. (Global Issues: Gender Equality and Women's Empowerment, n.d.) Yet, gender equality discourse does not limit to women alone, but on the relationship between men and women in the society.

Several studies have shown that the public policies have been based on the needs of the dominant group in society or on the needs of the decision-makers, mostly men. The women's rights movements, the development of gender studies and sex-disaggregated data, have all helped unveil the fact that public policies often did not take into account women's differing needs and situations. Evidently, decisions regarding public policies and services, which do not fully take into account the needs and situations of all final users may lead to inappropriate solutions and an inadequate allocation of public funds. (What is Gender Mainstreaming?, n.d.)

Governments and policy-makers have begun to recognise the demands for basic rights of women, transgender and other sexual and gender minorities. The governments have been compelled to give due attention to the strident voices of activism raised from a range of platforms and movements. There has also been a significant shift of focus from women being mere beneficiaries of government policies to that of being growth agents in India's political economy across all sectors. The role of women in the development process has shifted from Woman and Development (WAD) to Women's Empowerment and Agency (WEA).The concept of gender mainstreaming is the latest addition to this discourse on women empowerment.

Gender Mainstreaming

Gender mainstreaming is an approach to policy-making that takes into account both women's and men's interests and concerns. The concept of gender mainstreaming was first introduced at the 1985 Nairobi World Conference on Women. It was established as a strategy in international gender equality policy through the Beijing Platform for Action adopted at the 1995 Fourth United Nations World Conference on Women in Beijing, and subsequently adopted as a tool to promote gender equality at all levels.

In 1997, the United Nations Economic and Social Council (Gender Mainstreaming, n.d.) defined gender mainstreaming as: "It is a strategy for making women's as well as men's concerns and experiences an integral dimension of the design, implementation, monitoring and evaluation of policies and programmes in all political, economic and societal spheres so that women and men benefit equally and inequality is not perpetrated. The ultimate goal is to achieve gender equality." In 1998, the Council of Europe defined gender mainstreaming as: "The (re)organisation, improvement, development and evaluation of policy processes, so that a gender equality perspective is incorporated in all policies at all levels and at all stages, by the actors normally involved in policy-making". Women and men have different needs and living conditions and circumstances. The aim of gender mainstreaming is to take into account these differences when designing, implementing and evaluating policies, programmes and projects, so that they benefit both women and men and do not increase inequality but enhance gender equality. Gender mainstreaming aims to solve –sometimes hidden- gender inequalities. It is, therefore, a mechanism for achieving gender equality.

Gender Budgeting is the first tool for achieving gender mainstreaming. It entails dissection of government budget to establish its gender differential impacts. Gender Budgeting also ensures that gender commitments are translated in the budgetary commitments because adequate monetary allocations are very important for the achievement of desired outcomes.

Gender Mainstreaming: The Localised Meanings

Gender Mainstreaming comprise of gender-specific activities and affirmative action, whenever women or men are in a particularly disadvantageous position. Gender-specific interventions can target women exclusively, men and women together, or only men, to enable them to participate in and benefit equally from development efforts. These are necessary temporary measures designed to combat the direct and indirect consequences of past discrimination.

In India, there exists a wide gender inequality measured in terms of all the Gender Indices (GI) developed by UNDP. Economic review 2018 shows that (Board, 2018) the Gender Development Index (GDI) value of India is with low equality in human development achievements between women and men. The GDI measures gender gaps in human development achievements by accounting for disparities between women and men in health, knowledge and living standards. In terms of Gender Inequality Index

(GII) also, India ranks 127th with a GII value 0.524 (Board, 2018). GII measure gender inequalities in three important aspects of human development: (a) reproductive health, (b) empowerment, (c) economic status. In terms of "life-course gender gap" released by UNDP, India's position is in the "bottom third category". Life-course gender gap is measured by analyzing gender gaps in the choices and opportunities over health, education, labour market and work, political representation, time use and social protection.

Responding to this Indian context, where women are largely disadvantageous to men, gender mainstreaming policies focusing more on women. It is mostly done through policies for women empowerment which involve awareness raising, building self-confidence, expansion of choices, increased access to and control over resources and actions to transform the structures and institutions which reinforce and perpetuate gender discrimination and inequality.

Gender Status in Kerala

In comparison to other Indian states, Kerala is known for its gender development achievements. Economic review 2018 (Board, 2018) shows that women of Kerala having high health status in comparison to men in the State as well as to persons in other parts of the country. Most of the social indicators are highly favourable to women in the State.The indicators of female literacy, life expectancy, maternal mortality rate; adolescent birth rates and proportion of adult females with secondary education are impressive in Kerala. Kerala is a pioneer in ensuring 50 percent seats in Local Governments to women.

At the same time, the indicators of labour market participation, many of the lifestyle, health indicators are not favourable to Kerala women. According to the 68th Round of National Sample Survey, for the year 2011-12, a wide gap between male and female Labour Force Participation Rates (LFPRs) is seen in the State. The data on the sectoral distribution of employment in Kerala shows that a larger proportion of women are engaged in the agricultural sector, while the percentage share of males engaged in the service sector is much higher compared to females. Large numbers of women in the industry sector, are engaged in low productivity, labour intensive, less remunerated traditional industries like handlooms, Khadi, coir, cashew.

Contrary to the high social development, including high educational level, crime against women continues to be another major concern in Kerala.

The safety of the women in home and public place is a serious issue. Kerala is among the top ten States in terms of crime rates against women (National Crime Record Bureau, 2017). Increasing alcoholism and violence against women increasing stress on women and constraining the stress on women and the achievement of gender equality. So the development experience in Kerala suggests that the accomplishments in health and education are necessary but insufficient to support gender equality. Women in Kerala do not have equal access to economic opportunities and resources or equal voice and participation in political community decision-making. Given the unique and favourable human development context, Kerala is badly in need of a considered gender and development strategy to address the second generation of economic and political challenges of women.

Increasing suicides among men is another issue to be considered. More boys than girls are missing in tertiary levels and here is inadequate data to understand this phenomenon because there is no focus on boys or men of the gender equation. (Gender Budget Manual for Local Self Government Institutions of Kerala, 2017) Thus, while the predominant focus in development may continue to be on women, the state also recognises that there are male gender issues that cannot be ignored if gender equality and empowerment are to be achieved.The strategy needs to be developed through a democratic process, and herald in a shift from an approach of women's empowerment to one of gender equality. In defining this strategy, the time has also come to recognise that gender issue of men to be considered if gender equality is to progress in Kerala.The adoption Gender mainstreaming was happening in this context.

Gender Mainstreaming in Kerala

The Gender Equality and Women's Empowerment (GEWE) Policy 2015 is an updating of the policy on Women issued by the Kerala government in 2009 and shifts focus solely on women, to a more inclusive policy focusing on gender equality and rights.

The GEWE policy adopts gender mainstreaming as the key approach to achieving gender equality and recognises that men, along with women, need to be fully involved in the process of social transformation and change. According to Hindu newspaper report (Kerala Announces Gender Policy, 2015) dated 17th April, 2015, while the primary focus will continue to be on women empowerment and rights, the new policy recognises that there are emerging male gender issues that must also receive consideration to achieve gender equality. The new policy claimed to change of focus from women to gender and sought to involve men as well as women in its transformation agenda, recognising that issues like alcoholism and male violence are also to be taken on board.

The State government has decided to prioritise gender mainstreaming in all development policies and interventions. All departments/agencies which receive public funds need to prepare respective gender action plans.The policy establishes a process and accountability framework to design and monitor gender-informed development projects in the State. It envisaged the appointment of a person in each department to serve as a focal point on gender. Unlike the 2009 policy, which talked about allocating not less than 10% of the plan funds both at the state and local government levels, new policy aimed for the introduction of gender budgeting and auditing at state and local government levels, use of the Gender Board for monitoring gender projects at state and local levels, incorporation of gender auditing as a part of the state budget.

The Gender planning, auditing and budgeting manual (Gender Planning, Auditing and Budgetting Manual, 2015) that released by the social justice department to meet the Gender Equality and Women Empowerment policy recommendation explains the process of gender mainstream that is to be executed around various departments in Kerala.This manual asks all plans, policies and schemes should be viewed through a gender lens. It argues for a gender perspective to each phase of policy development.

The Gender planning, auditing and budgeting manual firstly argues for a thorough gender analysis based on sex disaggregated data in order to identify the barriers and constraints to gender equality in Kerala society. Secondly, all government departments are asked to set gender related objectives for the department. The next step involves identifying the solutions that need to be delivered to achieve objectives. In determining solution, the department can be incorporated civil society as suitable partners in addressing the solution. Next, each department is asked to classify all objectives into three categories based upon the nature of expenditures. Category A includes policies, programmes and schemes (PPS) are those where expenditure are wholly targeted to women. Category B consists of those PPS where between 1 to 99 percent is targeted to women. Category C includes those of PPS which deliver the general type of goods and service to the community. Typically, they constitute the bulk of Departments' PPS, and can benefit men and women differently. This largely happens due to the gender based barriers to participate in, and accessing, development benefits. Manual urges the departments to incorporate additional precautions in this category C to ensure that both women and men have equal access to these benefits. Each project, policy, scheme should specify the number of women and men who are expected to benefit from the spending. Gender resource person of each department is responsible for monitoring gender related outputs and outcomes for all their PPS. After evaluation, Department must prepare a brief Department Gender Action Plan.

Best Practices

In order to meet the outcome of GEWE policy, the Kerala government has envisaged multiple innovative programmes. The next session is brief review of some such major policies. Mainstreaming gender to achieve gender equality was the common aim of all these projects. Three best practices for women empowerment and gender equality are taken for the analysis. The data concerned is collected from official sites of The Kerala State women's Development Corporation Ltd. and Department of Social Justice, Government of Kerala.

Policies on Gender Equality

Gender Park

Gender Park was conceived by the Department of Social Justice, Government of Kerala. It acts as a convergence centre for State, Non-Government Organisations (NGO), academia and other stakeholders for gender-related education, activities, entrepreneurship, training and capacity development, in the spheres of Culture, Art, Literature and media, social, human, economic, and political development. The Park would provide a space for all gender identities, including transgender, to overcome the socio-economic and political boundaries imposed on them by society and contribute to the economic, cultural, and social aspects of the state and the country. Its mission is to conduct high-quality research and effective capacity development relevant to provide innovative, practical recommendations for policymakers and the public to foster just and inclusive societies for all.

Transgender Policy

Kerala is the first State in India which declared a Transgender Policy in 2015. The policy allows for the self-identification of a person as a Transgender. It also recommends the establishment of District-level Trans Gender Boards that issue identification cards to transgenders. Various schemes for the welfare of transgenders are being implemented. Transgender

Helpline (24x7) and crisis management centre was established. The government has initiated schemes for financial assistance for vocational training/ skill development for self-employment/regular employment, Pension for destitute transgender above the age of 60 years. A continuing literacy programme, Scholarship for transgender students, medical insurance, financial assistance for sex re-assignment surgery (SRS) and Short Stay Homes for Transgender were arranged as part of the project.

Sadhayiryam Munnottu

Sadhayiryam Munnottu is a State wide ongoing project started in the year 2018. It is basically a comprehensive gender awareness programme, which has been divided into two sectors. One is the awareness in the government departments, institutions, public sector and other work places like unorganised and informal sectors. The second sector covers the public and those interacting with the public, men, women, Transgender and other sexual and gender minorities. This awareness campaign has to reach all the areas like Kudumbhasree, ASHA workers, MGNREGA, School mid-day meal workers, ICDS workers including the homemakers. The awareness campaign will be carried out with the help of modules, skits, songs, *kalajadha*, poster exhibitions, video shows, short film festivals, bringing out small handbooks on topics like women and media, women and law, women and labour, women and society. These handbooks will be made as a part of the conscientisation programme. In the educational front, gender audit of textbooks will take place. All the schools will have sex-education classes for the high school be conducted. Awareness programmes with the help of Transgender Board will be conducted on Homophobia for the police whom would sometimes have to be done in police stations.

Policies on Women Empowerment

Nirbhaya

Nirbhaya Project mainly focuses on a three-point agenda: Prevention, Prosecution and Protection. Multiple intervention are aimed for sensitising society, empowering vulnerable groups and targeting contributing factors such as alcoholism, gender discrimination and consumerism.The policy focuses on formulation and implementation of strong laws in the areas of child abuse, commercial sexual exploitation and sex trafficking. Fast-Track Courts exclusively for women and children have been already established. The programme envisages setting up of Nirbhaya homes for sexually abused women.

She-Taxi

She Taxi is an innovative public-private partnership (PPP) that serves as a platform to promote a sustainable business model for the economic empowerment, safety and security of women through the promotion of entrepreneurship. She Taxis are driven by women, for women, and provide them with a safe means of transport. She Taxis are equipped with safety enabled technology that makes travelling safe and secure for both the driver and the passenger. Database of all Emergency Response Systems in the city, including police, ambulance, automobile workshops, fire force, safe night shelters for women and hospitals are available to the drivers, and she taxi vehicles are proactively monitored from a 24×7 Security Control Room.

She Stay, She Toilet, She Pad

She stay is a project that seek to provide safety and convenient accommodation to women who are living out of their homes in search of employment in big cities and urban and rural townships. The She toilet project in the state tries to tackle problems of female hygiene and access to sanitation in public spaces. It ensures that every woman has access to clean, hygienic and fully equipped women-friendly public toilets. The automatic, unmanned, she-toilet are based on cost- effective and environment friendly technology. She pad project helps the girl students to menstrual hygiene and management.Ensuring accessibility to affordable sanitary pads in the school premises will be the prime aim of this project.

Analysis

The erstwhile measures for women empowerment failed to solve the issue of gender inequality. Though efforts on empowering women need to be continued to reduce the gender gap and avoid discrimination, it cannot reach the goal of gender equality. In such a context, the idea of gender mainstreaming has its relevance as it is a strategy for making all gender concerns and experiences an integral dimension of the design, implementation, monitoring and evaluation of policies and programmes. But in Indian context, as the official data suggests, the idea of gender mainstreaming carries out as version of women empowerment.

In Kerala too the situation is not much different. Even with decades of women component planning, the development experience in Kerala suggests that the accomplishments in health and education are necessary but insufficient to support gender equality or women empowerment.

Feminisation of local governance in terms of enhancement of women's quota from 33% to 50% in all local government positions and the preeminent role played by the *Kudumbasree* women in Panchayat affairs have not resulted in the transformation of Women Component Planning to a gender responsive policies.

Though the idea of gender budgeting is part of the Kerala planning for last one decade, it still did not make much impact in gender empowerment. Studies (Eapen) suggest that the main weakness of efforts to implement the gender Budget methodology on real Budgets has been its limited ability, mainly due to non-availability of gender disaggregated data and the absence of a broader vision of including women in the development planning process. Including gender into Budgeting has to move beyond the numbers, to engage with the overall planning process and the extent to which there is adequate support for social investment and provision of public goods which are critical for women. It is necessary to focus on schemes depending on women's priorities, rather than finances and to then ensure that funds are made available for these schemes. This means we need to plan women specific projects in women unrelated sectors (largely infrastructure) to visibilise them in all sectors of development. It is necessary therefore to create awareness of its significance across Departments, even those which are apparently "gender unrelated".

In such a context, the concept of gender mainstreaming can be considered. Kerala can be a better laboratory for gender mainstreaming in India, as it is the place where women are in a better position and the difference between both genders are less in many fields. The Gender Equality and Women's Empowerment (GEWE) Policy 2015 is a good beginning in this regard. It is for the first time in the development history of Kerala, the concept of gender mainstream got representated in the policy document. Before it, our policy discussions on gender equality are only reached up to the idea of gender budgeting.

The concept of gender mainstreaming calls for positive action at different levels. Also, it requires commitment, capacities and resources. At the policy level, GEWE policy trying to ensure that the issue of gender equality becomes a visible and central concern in policy and planning. At the programme level, it seek that all interventions create opportunities for women's empowerment and facilitate gender equality. At the organisational level, the policy encourages to ensure that space and opportunities for learning and growth are created equally for women and men at all levels. Thus, gender mainstreaming strategy in GEWE policy was an effort to allocation of adequate resources for gender equality objectives that are built in to all strategy and policy documents, Equal participation of men and women in setting priorities and in all aspects of programming, Equality of opportunity as well as equality of outcome for women and men, through specifically addressing the constraints experienced by women.

As Nisha Velappan Nair and John S Moolakkattu rightly points out (Nisha Velappan Nair, 2018), Kerala initiated some innovative projects on women empowerment through introducing gender-friendly infrastructure in usually women-shy sectors such as public works, transport, and public offices in the form of construction of toilets, restrooms, and drinking water facilities for women, women's finishing schools for skill upgradation and improvement of employability, innovative housing scheme for low-paid women workers, working women's hostels, night shelters, and Nirbhaya programme for the rescue, restoration, and rehabilitation of women who are victims of sexual abuse, and fast-track courts to try cases emanating from Nirbhaya.

Above mentioned are some innovative projects on women empowerment, similar attention was lacking in case of men's issues. When we look into men friendly projects in present Kerala, the researcher could not find any exclusive policies oriented towards improvement of men. As men are the highest victims of alcoholism and drug abuse, Men must be the main stakeholders of project *Vimukti*, a state mission for a deaddiction project to conduct awareness campaigns against alcoholism and drug abuse among students and youth. Statistics show that young men of age group of 15 to 35 are the prime victims of road accidents in Kerala. So young men will be the main stakeholders of *Subhayathra*, the project aiming for comprehensive programme in road safety, traffic management and enforcement traffic rules.

Men self help group scheme in Kerala under *Swarnajayanthi Grama Swaroskar Yojana* (SGSY) is the only male exclusive policy. It aims to reduce rural unemployment and poverty. The policy of SGSY was replaced by central government with a new policy called National Rural Livelihood Mission (NRLM) in June 2011. Subsequently the Men SHGS formed, nurtured and functioned under SGSY have reduced their role, due to lack of provision for financial assistance to men groups in NRLM scheme. In order to overcome the crisis, the Kerala government has initiated an income generation programme for BPL self-help men groups under a new project. But it too was not impressive to the earlier policy. Men come under the perview of social security if they are aged, disabled, deviant, addicted or chronically ill. These need to be changed. Even while the predominant focus in development may continue to be on women, the state also recognises that there are male gender issues that cannot be ignored if gender equality and empowerment are to be achieved. So the studies to be conducted by shifting focus from women to questions of gender. The immediate and urgent focus is to be given in generating awareness and disseminate a sound understanding of gender concepts. *Gender Park, Sadhairyam Munnottu*, Transgender policy are some best practices Kerala can present to the world.

Though the idea of Gender Park was much promising, conceptually, even after six years of its existence, it is still an unfinished plan. Most of the novel ideas of *Gender Park* could not be executed yet. The early enthusiasm subsidised very soon. Similarly, *She taxi* has too failed to live up to its expectations. The lack of publicity, higher fare, entry of online services are considered as the main reasons for the programme to fail. The lack of online system for booking and the less number of cabs too have caused the decline of the system. Programmes under *Nirbhaya* seem to have had an episodic existence allegedly due to lack of enough state support.

Continuous monitoring and evaluation of all programmes at regular intervals, effective dissemination of concepts, efficient tools for the practical implementation and support from leaders will be crucial to ensure a strong and sustainable impact. Other factors are equally important to ensure proper gender mainstreaming, such as: political will, commitment to and awareness of gender equality issues, knowledge, resources (including expertise) and availability of information.

Conclusion

There is a need to develop a collective ownership of the gender equality or the women's empowerment agenda and for more people to become aware that a gender equality agenda is a vision, one that will protect both men and women. An approach to achieving gender equality should focus on both men and women. Women's empowerment is an essential first step before one can effectively implement gender equality. At the same time, it is important to recognise and better understand the decreasing enrollments of men in the primary and tertiary education levels and to examine the need to address this issue. It is important to bring men into this equation and garner their involvement in women's empowerment and gender equality. If the social change is to be harmoniously carried out, then men and other gender identities need to become part of the solution of the gender equation.

Gender mainstreaming is a responsibility of all actors and is relevant for all policy areas that deal with the needs of people and at all levels. Policy areas which at first sight do not seem relevant, might contain (hidden) aspects of gender inequality. Awareness must be raised to ensure a demand at the grassroots level for gender equality. While the government has a key responsibility in this regard, equal responsibility lies with other development partners such as NGOs and civil society representatives. The relevance of Gender Park and Sadhairyam Munnottu lies in this aspect.

Gender Park can be used to conduct high-quality research and effective capacity development relevant to provide innovative, practical recommendations for policymakers and the public to foster just and inclusive societies for all, in addition to educating students in gender theory and practice. The Sadhairym Munnottu project can be used to propagate awareness in the government departments, institutions, public sector and other work places like unorganised and informal sectors. Such intensive awareness programme using all state non-state paraphernalia is the need of the day, because it only can lead to society to alleviate from gender dogmas. Such a society, which think above patriarchy, gender binaries could only accommodate its transgender or non-gender communities. As we forget ourselves in the hype created by transgender policy, the academia should think about whether Kerala society is prepare enough to conceive the radical ideas of Transgender policy 2015 and should visualise the bridging programmes that may propagate gender awareness around the society, otherwise every policy with all its innovative spirit remain as mere cosmetic attempt.

References

Board, S. P. (2018). *Economic Review 2018.* Thiruvanandhapuram: Government of Kerala.

Eapen, D. M. (n.d.). *Gender Responsive Budgeting: Enhancing integration of Gender Perspective in Relevant Government Programmes/schemes:Documenting Kerala's Experience* . Kerala State Planning Board.

(2017). *Gender Budget Manual for Local Self Government Institutions of Kerala.* Thrissur: Kerala Institute of Local Administration.

Gender Mainstreaming. (n.d.). Retrieved from UN Women: https://www.unwomen.org/en/how-we-work/un-system-coordination/gender-mainstreaming

(2015). *Gender Planning, Auditing and Budgetting Manual.* Goverment of Kerala.

Global Issues: Gender Equality and Women's Empowerment. (n.d.). Retrieved from Peace corps: https://www.peacecorps.gov/educators/resources/global-issues-gender-equality-and-womens-empowerment/

(2015). *Kerala Announces Gender Policy.* Thiruvananthapuram: The Hindu.

Nisha Velappan Nair, J. S. (2018). *Gender-Responsive Budgeting: The Case of a Rural Local Body in Kerala.* Sage.

What is Gender Mainstreaming? (n.d.). Retrieved from Council of Europe Portal: https://www.coe.int/en/web/genderequality/what-is-gender-mainstreaming.

15

Right to Health of Transgender People: Issues and Concerns

— *Rajagopal, P.K.*

Abstract

Transgender people have been there in every society, ethnicity and class since the beginning of recorded human history. Transgender community remains as one of the most marginalised communities as they belong to another category than the common gender, 'male' or 'female' conceptions. Hence they have to suffer enormous problems emerging out of social ostracism and discrimination. Lack of proper education facilities, employment and healthcare facilities are the other constraints they have to confront with. There have been certain positive steps from the part of the authorities for the well-being of the transgender community in recent years, but they feel them as inadequate and want much more to do in the fight for equality.

Lesbian, gay, bisexual, or transgender (LGBT) people are members of our society facing series of human rights and health-related issues. Transgender people composed of all races and ethnicities and belong to all ages and socio-economic status. The term 'transgender people' is commonly used to describe people who violate social gender norms. They are a different group of people from the gender assigned to them at birth. Sex designated at birth is based on the appearance of the external genitalia and is recorded accordingly on the birth certificate. Cultures, regions, and gender over time have conceptualised transgender people in different ways. *Transgender* is often used as an umbrella term to signify individuals who defy rigid, dual gender constructions, and who express or present a breaking of culturally prevalent stereotypical gender roles. Transgender people may live full or part-time in the gender role 'opposite' to their biological sex[1]. In India, about one-third of the transgender people live in Maharashtra, Delhi,

Uttar Pradesh, Odisha, West Bengal, formerly undivided Andhra Pradesh and Tamil Nadu.

Transgender Rights and Social Impacts

Human rights are basic rights of human beings regardless of gender, religious identity or nationality. Transgender people are human beings and so their rights are to be protected. The human rights issues they face in the civilised society include unemployment, lack of education and medical facilities, discrimination, stigma towards HIV infected persons and problems related to marriage and adoption that invite adequate attention. An NGO in Kerala conducted a study on the status of the transgender community which revealed that the dropout rate of transgender students is very high in the educational sector. Severe harassment, poverty, lack of special quota or reservation, negative home environment are the other issues prevailed[2]. In 1994, transgender people were given the right to vote in India, but the question of giving them voter identity cards remains as a challenge before the authorities. Many of them were denied ID cards with their sex category. Other area of concern to the transgender community is with regard to property rights and child adoption. They are often pushed to the periphery as a social phenomenon and so many pursue begging and dancing for their living. Sometimes all the options to feed themselves are exhausted, they engage themselves as sex workers for survival. The option as sex worker is very dangerous and may become disastrous as it results in serious health issues like HIV infection. In a 2014 judgment, the Supreme Court directed the Centre and State governments to implement HIV surveillance systems for the transgender community to protect their health[3].

Employment

Transgender people have very limited employment opportunities. As per 2011 census data, India's transgender population counts to 4, 90,000 people, out of which only a microscopic minority could have obtained proper employment. The National Human Rights Commission's study of transgender rights provides a clear picture of the transgender situation in the country. According to the study, 92% of transgender people lose the right to participate in any type of economic activity in the country, even those eligible were denied to work. In 2017, 23 transgender people were employed at Kochi Metro Rail Limited in Kerala, but eight of them quit their jobs within a month due to denial of proper accommodation facilities. Such discrimination at work place is actually a violation of the basic human right of the transgender population which is to be redressed.

Healthcare

Transgender individuals have specific healthcare needs. They may have behavioural health concerns and they are also at higher risk of developing health problems. Due to low employment rates, lack of insurance coverage, or fear of discrimination, these people have less accessibility to healthcare. An important issue in this regard is to find a healthcare provider who knows how to treat transgender people. Also, these people often hesitate to uncover their health history, hormone treatment etc., to the healthcare provider. Transgender persons may be at greater risk for heart attack, stroke and lung diseases. This is due to hormone use, along with cigarette smoking and alcohol consumption, high blood pressure and diabetes. Due to hormone treatment, there may be chances of developing cancer also. Besides, there is the risk for sexually transmitted infections (STIs), depression etc.

They have no access to public spaces like bathrooms and toilets; similar situations are there in hospitals, schools and work places. They have to face physical and verbal abuses, forced sex, theft of money and property and some sort of social ostracism. They are widely discriminated in the healthcare sphere also; registering them as 'men' and entering men's wards, verbal abuse by hospital staff and co-patients were reported.

Transgender and Sexual Rights

Sexual health is a state of physical, mental and social well-being in relation to sexuality. The World Health Organisation (WHO) defines sexual health as physical, emotional, psychological and social well-being concerning sex; it is not simply the absence of disease, inadequacy, or weakness, but also associated with pleasurable and safe sexual experiences, without compulsion, discrimination or violence[4]. Sexual health cannot be achieved without respecting certain human rights. Sexual rights are some of the human rights recognised in international and national human rights documents and other international law agreements relating to the realisation of sexual health. Sexuality is a natural and valuable part of human life, an essential part of humanity. To achieve high standards of health, they must be empowered to make choices in their sexual and reproductive rights and be safe in expressing their sexual identity[5].

Transgender community have also sexual needs that are similar to that of non-trans people. They sometimes engage in unsafe sex and thus become victims of sexually transmitted diseases (STD). In the last decade, social awareness and acceptance of the transgender community have been considerably increased. A transgender person does not have a gender identity similar to that given at birth. Transgender status does not correlate with a person's sexual orientation[6].

Transgender and HIV Infection

HIV continues to be a major global public health problem that has stolen the lives of millions of people around the world. HIV can be transmitted from different sources such as HIV-infected mothers, by direct contact with HIV-infected body fluids such as blood, sperm and vaginal fluids etc. Human Immune Deficiency Virus (HIV) targets the immune system of human beings and weakens their immunity against infections. By the end of 2018, approximately 37.9 million people were living with HIV in the world.

The total number of people infected with HIV (PLHIV) in India is estimated to be 21.40 lakh (15.90 lakh - 28.39 lakh) in 2017, making it the third-largest affected country in the world. Most infections are caused by heterogeneous transmission. Drug use is a major driver of the HIV epidemic in the Northeast of India[7]. Sex work continues to be the most important source of HIV infection in India, as a large number of clients are affected by sex workers. Although female sex workers were the epicentre of the epidemic in the early days, that have been concentrated in the migrant population, including men who have sex with men (MSM), intravenous drug users (in the north-eastern states of Manipur, Nagaland, Delhi and Punjab) etc.[8]

Table 1: Main Routes of HIV Transmission in India up to 2013

Sl. No.	*Category*	*Percentage*
1.	Heterosexual	85.6
2.	Homosexual/bisexual	1.4
3.	Parent to child	5.9
4.	Blood and blood products	1.1
5.	Infected needles and syringes	1.3
6.	Not known	4.7

Source: Paranjape, R.S & Challacombe, S.J,(2016), HIV/AIDS in India: an overview of the Indian epidemic, Retrieved from https://doi.org/10.1111/odi.12457

India has recently embarked on an HIV prevention strategy that is strongly associated with lower rates of infection in low and high risk groups[9]. Several studies have been conducted to identify high-risk groups of HIV-infected people, such as injecting drug users, having sex with men, and identifying key groups, such as female sex workers (FSW) and transgender groups. Among the high risk groups, transgender group has the highest HIV infection rate (8.82%). See table 2.

Table 2: HIV infection (%) among high risk behaviour groups in India (2010–2011)

Sl.No.	*Category*	*Percentage*
1	Migrants	0.99
2	Truckers	2.59
3	Female sex workers	2.67
4	Men who have sex with men	4.43
5	Injecting drugs users	7.14
6	Transgender	8.82

Source: Paranjape, R.S & Challacombe, S.J, (2016), HIV/AIDS in India: an overview of the Indian epidemic, Retrieved from https://doi.org/10.1111/odi.12457

Despite many years of research on HIV / AIDS and the population it affects, very little is known about transgender people and HIV. In the vast majority of studies, transgender people consider sex as a birthmark, which not only discounts their identities, but is relatively invisible to public health officials and advocacy organisations working on prevention, treatment and HIV-related healthcare[10].

Transgender people are becoming a high-risk HIV group. In India, it is acknowledged that transgender people have unique needs and concerns and that it is better to view them as a separate group that does not fall under the category of "MSM". In 2014, UNAIDS published a study report which revealed that majority of transgender people in India are engaging in sex work and the rate of HIV prevalence is very high among this group compared to others i.e., up to nine times higher than non-transgender female sex workers[11]. Studies pointed out the reality that transgender sex workers are engaging in unprotected sex not using condoms, which makes them highly vulnerable to HIV. It is a fact that unrestrained use of drugs and alcohol make these people engaging in unsafe sexual activities. The transgender people commonly use injectable hormones for gender enhancement and usually they do the injecting themselves. Such practices involves in a high risk of HIV transmission as there is the possibility of sharing needles with others[12].

A few recent studies that consider transgender women (even transgender men) as a separate group reveal a dangerously high rate of HIV infection among them. According to a recent international analysis, transgender women are 49 times more likely to be infected with HIV compared to the general population. Although transgender men are less likely to be HIV-positive than transgender women, their rates of infection are still higher than the general population.

The Centres for Disease Control and Prevention (CDC) suggests that certain risk factors that are directly linked to transphobia and the marginalisation that transgender people face can lead to higher rates of infection. These risk factors include; high rates of drug, alcohol abuses, sex work, internment, homelessness, suicide attempts, unemployment, lack of family support, violence, stigma, discrimination, limited healthcare access and health-related conflicts. They live in a society where there is considerable stigma and discrimination against transgender people, pushing them into situations that increase their risk of HIV and severely limiting their ability to have adequate care once they are infected.

Transgender people confronts with greater barriers to healthcare that other HIV-infected people may not have, especially the fear of being discriminated against by healthcare professionals or denied treatment due to their gender identity or expression. These barriers reduce the chances of transgender people being screened for HIV and continuing to receive HIV-related medical care. In addition to the high rates of harassment experienced by transgender people, they have higher rates of sexual violence than the general population and other groups in the LGBT community. Transgender people are less likely to report an attack to the police or to go to hospitals for post-assault care for the fear of further harassment. Transgender people who are discriminated against at work or who are unable to pursue advanced education due to intimidation or harassment at school are more likely to engage in high-risk sex work, more likely to be infected with HIV and other sexually transmitted infections (STIs).The fear of abuse and discrimination makes them hesitate in accessing sexual health services. Their experiences are often classified as a psychological disorder; this is one of the difficulties they face when accessing health services.

Prevent and reduce HIV transmission through targeted programming of education and awareness among targeted groups and take initiatives to reduce new cases. HIV preventive measures have been successfully implemented among the transgender people in India. Primary healthcare providers are to be provided with adequate training to understand and respond to the health needs of transgender people. The requirements for HIV prevention in transgender people are different. Transgender people need to be included in studies of HIV-infected communities and HIV /

AIDS advocates need to acknowledge the ways in which HIV transmits to transgender people. Transgender people need access to qualified, affirmative, sex-positive, and safer-sex information specifically geared to their body, relationships and community concerns[13].

Many countries in the world do not recognise the rights of transgender people and often deny passports and other identity documents to them. Violence against transgender people are increasingly reported in different parts of the country. It is estimated that about 20 million transgender people are living in India. The two-judge Supreme Court Bench headed by Justice K.S. Radhakrishnan empathised with the transgender people and remarked that they should also be treated as a minority group i.e., "socially and economically backward" for enabling them to achieve quota in work and educational fields. The judges directed the government to ensure medical facilities such as special wards and special toilets for these people are available in hospitals[14]. These directions of the apex court have become a relief to the transgender community. The needs of transgender people should be regularly considered in public health efforts to improve the overall health of each individual and eliminate health inequalities. Social programmes must be formulated for the holistic development of the transgender community, thus empowering and improving them.

As a result of the continuous efforts of activists over the past several years, the Hon'ble Supreme Court of India in 2014 has issued an important decree in the case of *National Legal Services Authority v. Union of India*. The Court noted that discrimination and misbehaviour with the transgender community is common in India, particularly in the education and employment sectors. As a result, the Court has endorsed the rights to life of the third sex, which is included in Article 21 [1] of the Constitution. In an effort to provide legislative support for the recommendations made by the National Legal Services Authority of India, the Transgender Persons (Rights Protection) Bill, 2016 (Bill) has been drafted. On July 19, 2019, the Minister for Social Justice and Empowerment introduced the Transgender Persons (Protection of Rights) Bill, 2019 in Lok Sabha and it became the Transgender Persons (Protection of Rights) Act, 2019 on December 5, 2019. The Act aims to end discrimination against transgender persons in accessing education, employment and healthcare. It also recognises the right to self-perceived gender identity and provides for certification from a District Magistrate; in case a transgender person has had a gender-change surgery, the law says they can obtain a certificate from the medical facility where they had the operation, and apply for a change in their certificate[15].

Though the bill provides for the protection of transgender interests by preventing discrimination in employment, the implementation of such provisions is a great challenge. A strong legal mechanism is needed to protect transgender interests and criminals / violators are to be imposed with heavy fines. In addition, relevant amendments are needed to such legislations as the Equal Pay, Maternity Benefit and Employee State Insurance are to be amended to include the transgender persons within their purview. The provisions of the Bill should be strictly enforced to protect a transgender person from discrimination in the workplace.

Also, it is the need of the hour to create job opportunities for transgender people in order to provide a holistic atmosphere in our society. To achieve such a goal, the government can encourage the employers to hire transgender individuals. The government should take special attention that employers are submitting quarterly returns including the number of vacancies available, interviews conducted for them, and the number of filled-in vacancies and the percentage of transgender employed. Legal governance, as analyzed above, can do much. Empowering the transgender community by making workplaces more transgender-inclusive will not only reduce discrimination against them but assist them to be a part of India's economic growth.

Suggestions

The suggestions of the study in a nutshell:

1. An effective legal mechanism is needed for protecting the interests of the trans community and for criminalising the acts of discrimination towards transgender people.
2. Adequate amendments should be made to the relevant welfare legislations to include the transgender persons' requirements.
3. The government should take special attention to create sufficient employment opportunities to the transgender people.
4. Effective steps should be taken to combat HIV transmission among transgender people. NGOs should be entrusted with the mission of ensuring health rights and social justice for the transgender people.
5. Create awareness among the transgender community about the need for safer-sex to protect them from HIV.
6. The transgender community should be enabled to access healthcare services indiscriminately.

7. Above all, the attitude of the general public towards the transgender people may have to be changed; their sentiments and requirements may be amply respected.

The transgender community still faces discrimination even after legislative and judicial safeguards. The social welfare department provides a variety of social welfare schemes for the social and economic backward classes. But, there are no special plans for transgender people, except for rare cases. Andhra Pradesh and Tamil Nadu governments introduced several welfare measures for transgender people. The Tamil Nadu has formed Transgender Women's Welfare Board to address the social welfare issues of transgender people. Unfortunately, most transgender communities do not know much about the social welfare programmes available to them. It is the need of the hour to have an inclusive approach towards the transgender communities for redressing their discomfiture. The triple E approach (Education, Empowerment and Enlighten) is needed for their empowerment.

References

1. Chakrapani, V. (2010). *Hijras/Transgender Women in India*, UNDP, Retrieved from https://www.undp.org/content/dam/india/docs/hijras_transgender_in_india_hiv_human_rights_and_social_exclusion.pdf.
2. Transgender Survey of Kerala-2014-15, Sangama,Ernakulam Retrieved from http://swd.kerala.gov.in/DOCUMENTS/Report/Survey%20Report/12157.pdf.
3. *National Legal Service Authority Vs Union of India & Others* on April 15, 2014, Retrieved from https://indiankanoon.org/docfragment/193543132/?formInput=transgender
4. WHO.(2006). *Sexual and Reproductive Health*, Retrieved from https://www.who.int/reproductivehealth/topics/sexual_health/sh_definitions/en.
5. IPPF, *Sexual Rights: An IPPF Declaration*, Retrieved from https://www.ippf.org/resource/sexual-rights-ippf-declaration
6. Hormone Health Network. (2020). *Transgender Health*, Hormone.org, Endocrine Society, April 3, 2020, Retrieved from https://www.hormone.org/your-health-and-hormones/transgender-health.
7. NACO. (2010). *Annual Report -2009-10*, Department of AIDS Control Ministry of Health and Family Welfare Government of India, NACO.
8. Paranjape, R.S & Challacombe, S.J, (2016). *HIV/AIDS in India: An Overview of the Indian Epidemic*, Retrieved from https://doi.org/10.1111/odi.12457
9. *Ibid.*
10. Human Rights Campaign, *Transgender People and HIV: What We Know*, Retrieved from https://www.hrc.org/resources/transgender-people-and-hiv-what-we-know
11. UNAIDS (2014). *Prevention Gap Report.*

12. Herbst, J.H., Jacobs, E.D., Finlayson, T.J., et al. (2008). *Estimating HIV Prevalence and Risk Behaviors of Transgender Persons in the United States: A Systematic Review*, AIDS Behaviour 12, 1–17, Retrieved from https://doi.org/10.1007/s10461-007-9299-3.
13. Human Rights Campaign, op.cit.
14. *National Legal Service Authority vs Union of India*, op.cit.
15. Damini Nath, (2020). *Transgender Persons Act comes into effect*, The Hindu, January 11.

16

Financial Transaction Unsettled for Third Gender

— Karthika, K. and Nikhil, S.

Abstract

Third gender or Transgender are those people who have a gender identity that is different from their assigned sex. The Government of Kerala has introduced a couple of programmes for promoting transgender. Most of the programmes intended to empower them with financial stability. But, it is necessary to check their investment targets to ensure that whether they are having the capability to uplift their financial position. This study intends to know the socio-economic profile and financial preferences of transgender. It also studies their influencing factor in investment decisions. The result shows that transgender were least concern about financial management in their life. The study reveals that financial preferences have no relationship with their education and number of dependents.

Keywords: *Transgender, Finance, Investment, Savings.*

1. Introduction

An individuals' wellbeing depends on environment (home or family, school and media or information), culture (social valuation of parenting, teachers and education), people with whom one is dealing and even biological changes such as fetal programming, early development and immune system setting. Apart from this, the educational background and work experience will promote a person's wellbeing to a great extent. Wellbeing is a broader term as it includes the overall growth of an individual but as far as transgender is concerned, the concept of third gender itself is in progressing stage. So, before studying the wellbeing of transgender, there is a necessity to develop and promote this category of individuals in a step by step manner to improve their financial planning. Then only the efforts of the government and other local authorities will be fruitful.

The Government of Kerala trying to improve the lifestyle of transgender by providing platforms in various fields such as Beauty pageant for trans-women, a School for transgender in Kochi, Free sex reassignment surgeries and introduced the concept of G-taxis operated by transgender. The Kerala State Sports Council has also organised first state-level sports meet. These initiations showed that the government has given utmost interest for the development of third gender and they focus to make them independent. Mere sanctioning of exclusive programmes will not find the right sense of development for them. It is highly necessary for an individual to be equipped to manage finance to uplift oneself to reach the level of financial independence. Financially a person is independent will pave way to be confident enough to lead a better life.

This study intends to analyze whether transgender has taken the matter of managing the funds seriously by analyzing their investment preferences.

2. Objectives of the Study

1. To understand the socio-economic profile of transgender and their financial preferences on investment.
2. To identify the factors that influence transgender to make investment decisions.

3. Statement of the Problem

An individual's financial soundness depends on one's financial capability and planning for the future. A couple of studies revealed gender differences in the financial well-being but seldom studies have been undertaken to know the financial preferences and investment decisions of transgender. This gap in the research intends to do the study focused on third gender.

4. Methodology of the Study

The study has been done through collecting primary data from transgender who were working at Trivandrum city. Out of 150 populations, 70 samples have responded promptly and convenience sampling has been used.

Objective I: Socio-economic Profile of Transgender and their Financial Preferences on Investment

Table 4.1: Classification on the basis of educational qualification

Educational qualification	*No. of transgender*	*Percent*
Up to HSC	40	57.0
Degree or above	30	43.0
Total	**70**	**100.0**

Source: Primary Data.

Inference: Majority (57%) of the transgender considered for the study was undergraduates but still near to an average (43%) were graduates.

Table 4.2: Type of organisation transgender employed

Organisation	*No. of transgender*	*Percent*
Private	50	71.0
Government	20	29.0
Total	**70**	**100.0**

Source: Primary Data.

Inference: The Table 4.2 reflects that out of 70 transgender, 71% employed in private organisation and 29% belongs to government organisation.

Table 4.3: Appointments into government services before or after 2017

Appointment	*No. of transgender*	*Percent*
After 2017	15	75.0
Before 2017	5	25.0
Total	**20**	**100.0**

Source: Primary Data.

Inference: Table 4.3 shows that out of 20 transgender who were working in the government organisation, 75% were appointed after 2017 reforms done by the Government of Kerala and only 25% before 2017. From this, it can be inferred that initiatives taken by the Government of Kerala has reduced the under employment and unemployment of this category.

Table 4.4: Link of educational qualification and the decision for consumption and investment

Educational Qualification	*Ratio of consumption and investment*				*Total*
	80:20	*60:40*	*50:50*	*20:80*	
Up to HSC	20	8	8	4	40
Degree or above	14	8	8	0	30
Total	**34**	**16**	**16**	**4**	**70**

Source: Primary Data.

Inference: A significant link between education and decision for consumption and investment cannot be identified. Irrespective of educational background, transgender were least bothered about their investment and give a significant proportion for consumption.

Table 4.5: Link of Number (No.) of dependents and the decision for consumption and investment

No. of dependents	*Ratio of consumption and investment*				*Total*
	80:20	*60:40*	*50:50*	*20:80*	
Nil	18	2	6	0	26
1	6	2	4	2	14
2	2	6	2	0	10
Above 2	8	6	4	2	20
Total	**34**	**16**	**16**	**4**	**70**

Source: Primary Data.

Inference: The relation between number of dependents and decision for consumption and investment were insignificant. Table 4.5 shows that transgender were not concerned about the proportion of investment out of their income as their dependents increase.

Table 4.6: High or low amount of investment preferred

Amount of investment	*No. of transgender*	*Percent*
High	28	40.0
Low	42	60.0
Total	**70**	**100.0**

Source: Primary Data.

Inference: The Table 4.6 shows that transgender prefer for low amount of investment than high amount. This shows that they do not give much importance to long term investment plans which is a prerequisite for better living conditions.

Objective II: Factors Influenced to Take Investment Decision

Table 4.7: Influencing factors in investment decision

Level of influence	*Family members*	*Relatives*	*Professional association*	*Educational Qualification*
Extremely influenced	5.70	5.70	0	28.60
Influenced	42.90	34.30	11.40	37.00
No opinion	31.40	40.00	45.80	28.60
Not influenced	14.30	11.40	31.40	2.90
Extremely not influenced	5.70	8.60	11.40	2.90
Total	**100.0**	**100.0**	**100.0**	**100.0**

Source: Primary data.

Inference: Table 4.7 shows that while making investment decisions, transgender believe that they were mostly influenced by their educational qualification whereas an average influence was done by family members. It is interesting to note that Professional associations were not at all influencing them and therefore it can be inferred that professional associations or expert advice has a limited role to improve the financial decision capability of transgender.

Table 4.8: Influence of print and visual media in investment decision

Level of influence	*Percent of transgender influenced*		
	Newspaper	*Television*	*Internet*
Extremely influenced	14.3	0	2.9
Influenced	34.3	28.6	28.6
No opinion	31.4	34.3	31.4
Not influenced	14.3	25.7	22.9
Extremely not influenced	5.7	11.4	14.3
Total	**100.0**	**100.0**	**100.0**

Source: Primary Data.

Inference: Transgender reveals that they depend on newspaper to get information on various investment avenues and to take financial decisions. In sequel to it, they depend on information from internet.

Table 4.9: Ranking of factors that lead to investment plan

Factors	*No. of transgender*	*Weighted score*	*Rank*
Return	13	278	3
Safety	16	352	1
Risk	11	231	4
Tax benefit	6	128	6
Liquidity	9	180	5
Future needs	15	308	2
Total	**70**	-	-

Source: Primary Data.

Inference: The Table 4.9 shows that safety is the major factor that will be considered while making an investment plan of transgender. After that, they prefer future needs followed by return on investment, risk and liquidity. As their earning capacity is not stable, they may be least concern about tax benefit that can be availed while making investments.

Table 4.10: Initiatives recommended to create awareness about the investment

Initiatives	*Yes*		*No*		*Total*
	No. of transgender	*Per cent*	*No. of transgender*	*Per cent*	
Training programmes	46	65.7	24	34.3	70
Advertisement	8	11.4	62	88.6	70
Workshops & seminar	24	34.3	46	65.7	70
Social welfare programmes	28	40.0	42	60.0	70

Source: Primary Data.

Inference: Table 4.10 shows that the initiatives to be taken for creating awareness about the investment among transgender. 65.7% opined that there is a need to conduct the training programmes to create awareness. 34.3% and 40.0% of the transgender were opined that there is a need to conduct workshops & seminars and social welfare programmes respectively.

5. Conclusion

Independence of a person in financial transactions defines ones' ability to live with confidence and to attain a better life. As far as transgender were concerned, in spite of various reforms from the part of the government, a real effort has to be done from the side of transgender for their upliftment. Even if, the government and welfare organisations provide various platforms to earn income, unless and until they know to manage the finance, development of third gender in real sense won't happen.

While planning their investment pattern, it is mentioned that they prioritise safety and future needs but seldom have they given importance for long term investments. Such contradictions were evident throughout the results. This reveals that no proper planning has been done by these categories of people by organising a proper financial transaction that provides them to lead a better life.

References

1. Chattopadhyay, Suhrid Sankar. (2015). "Transgender at the top" in *Front Line,* June 26.
2. Maji, Priyadarshini. (2017). "Goal based investing and its benefits" in *Business Today*, August 30.
3. https://www.indiatimes.com/specials/transgender-project/11-times-kerala-stepped-up-to-promote-transgender-rights-350704.html ....

Index

D

E

F

G

T

U